Thirty Days with E. Stanley Jones

Becky:
In Christ,

Global Preacher, Social Justice Prophet

John E. Harnish

To learn more about this book and its author, please visit
ThirtyDaysWith.com and JohnEHarnish.com

Cover design and illustration by Rick Nease
www.RickNeaseArt.com

Published by
Front Edge Publishing
42807 Ford Road, Suite 234
Canton, MI, 48187

Front Edge Publishing books are available for discount bulk purchases for events, corporate use and small groups. Special editions, including books with corporate logos,
personalized covers and customized interiors are available for purchase. For more information, contact Front Edge Publishing at info@FrontEdgePublishing.com.

HARNISH

I COMMEND MY JESUS TO YOU

I dedicate this book to the remembrance of my father,
Sylvester C. Harnish, who truly lived his faith and requested that the
words of E. Stanley Jones be carved on his tombstone:
"I commend my Jesus to you."

Special thanks to Clifford Bath, whose steadfast encouragement and
generous support helped make this book possible.

Contents

Advance Praise

I like this, a LOT! This is exactly the kind of book that E. Stanley Jones would write. The style speaks plainly with the opportunity for an appropriate response. Stanley would be pleased.
Dr. Robert Tuttle, author of *In Our Time: The Life and Ministry of E. Stanley Jones*

E. Stanley Jones was one of the five or six persons who played a most significant role in my Christian faith and journey. I spent a week with him at his ashram, then traveled with him for two weeks. I am grateful to Dr. Harnish for providing this 30 day experience with "Brother Stanley." I guarantee you will be impacted and challenged in your thoughts and actions.
Dr. Maxie Dunnam, President Emeritus Asbury Theological Seminary

I absolutely loved the format of this book! It provides a concise introduction to this remarkable person. However, the real gift is to make E. Stanley's thought and ministry relevant to our present day lives. It's a book that will enrich you for months and years to come.
Bishop Grant Hagiya, Los Angeles Area of the United Methodist Church

I remember the pure joy of reading *The Christ of Every Road* as a teen-ager in Estonia when religious books were banned. Some people managed to hide copies and shared them with us. Jones was one of my spiritual mentors in the midst of the openly atheist society. Jack Harnish offers valuable insights into the rich spiritual heritage which seeks mutual understanding based on the values of the Kingdom of God.

Dr. Meeli Tankler, Former Rector of the Baltic Methodist Theological Seminary, Tallinn, Estonia

E. Stanley Jones was one of the world's most influential Christians of the 20th century. Harnish taps into the heart of his life and ministry in this accessible resource. I recommend it to all Christians who want to glimpse what it takes to follow Christ in a multi-religious community.

Dr. Jack Jackson, E. Stanley Jones Associate Professor of Evangelism, Mission and Global Methodism, Claremont School of Theology

This is a compelling, fresh interpretation of one of the most influential missionary-statesman of the 20th century. It briefly and beautifully reflects upon the mission models and thought of E. Stanley Jones and provides new insights on the way we understand and imitate Jones in following the Lord Jesus Christ in our own times.

Dr. Shivraj Mahendra, Dean of Online Studies and Asst. Professor of World Christianity, New Theological College, Editor of History, Asian-American Theological Forum, Ordained Elder Free Methodist Church of India

This book is unlike most every devotional book I have ever seen: it both warms the heart and instructs the mind. E. Stanley Jones would like this book, and I think you will too.

Dr. Stephen Gunter, Director of E. Stanley Jones Professorships and Teaching Evangelist, Foundation for Evangelism

Our voice in the present is diminished when separated from the voices in the past. The voice of E. Stanley Jones is one voice we need to hear singing today. I consider Brother Stanley as the overall influence of my Christian life. I am so thankful that Jack Harnish has allowed me to hear his voice in these pages of this book.

Dr. Steve Harper, author, retired United Methodist Elder and professor of Spiritual Formation and Wesley Studies, Florida Annual Conference

This book clearly demonstrates that the message of E. Stanley Jones will never be dated, because it is a message about the Lord of yesterday, today and forever. At the same time, it tells many winsome stories, bringing Jones' life into new focus for the modern reader. Recommended for reading and study.

Rev. Dr. Jennifer Woodruff Tait, editor *Christian History Magazine* and priest, St. John's Episcopal Church, Corbin, Kentucky

It is indeed a joy and honor to read *Thirty Days with E. Stanley Jones*. In its 31 chapters, different aspects of Jones' life and work are described with insights and implications for us in our time and place, so it becomes a valuable resource for both academic research and meditation. I wholeheartedly endorse this work of great value and significance for all Christians.

Dr. Naveen Rao, Principal, Leonard Theological College, Jabalpur, India

Jack Harnish has written a powerful devotional book. The influence of E. Stanley Jones on his life and the lives of many shines through in a wonderful way. It honors Jones' legacy. I deeply respect this project and look forward to its impact.

Rev. Dr. Bill Moore, retired campus minister, pastor and conference council director, Lexington KY

The renowned Methodist missionary, E. Stanley Jones, was a global Christian. We need people like this in our world today more than ever. Like John Wesley, he viewed all the world as his parish. Jack Harnish provides a devotional introduction to this towering figure that both challenges and inspires. In this 30-day journey, Harnish offers you an opportunity to meet a true spiritual friend and mentor. His readings about "Brother Stanley" provide guidance for making your faith real as you travel your own road.

Dr. Paul Chilcote, Director of Center for Global Wesleyan Theology, Cambridge, England

John Harnish has done an outstanding work in putting into words the true essence of the remarkable E. Stanley Jones. His way of weaving in Jones' quotes and prayers bring to life the rich soul and spirit of the man. It is a book that is truly enriching and inspiring and brings a word we desperately need in our world today.

Betty Shannon Cloyd, former Director of the Upper Room Prayer Center and missionary to the Congo and to the Navajo People

I really liked the suggestions for small groups and hope to use them. A reader truly comes to feel a kinship with Jones. It's biography, it's devotional, it's history, all presented in an easily read format that led me to want to read more of Jones' books. Congratulations on completing a monumental task so well.

Dianne Stephenson, Adult Education, St. Andrews Presbyterian Church, Beulah, MI

Foreword

"Honesty is the best policy." Whether Benjamin Franklin coined the expression or not, it is a good principle to live by. So, in the interest of honest clarity, it is incumbent on me to confess, I have never been a great admirer of 'devotional' books. The reason for this is probably more complicated than I imagine, but of this I am aware. John Wesley warned his early Methodists, at the height of the Evangelical Revival in England, that some of his more fervent preachers were guilty of transmitting "more heat than light" to their followers. This was not a unique Methodist malady, but Wesley warned incessantly that a warm heart must be conjoined to a clear mind. For this reason, his published homilies of instruction to the early Methodists were characterized by clear doctrinal admonitions on the "way of salvation." The sermons were in essence theological lessons to live by.

Shaped in the womb of holiness Methodism, E. Stanley Jones's writings exemplify this foundational Wesleyan principle: his stories (and his own personal biography) warm the heart, but they are without fail informed by sound scriptural principles. In their very essence, Jones' writings are theological lessons to live by. That is why I love Jones's writings, and that is why I enthusiastically accepted the invitation from Rev. John E. Harnish to write a commendation and foreword for this book. This book is *unlike* most every devotional book I have ever seen: it both warms the heart and instructs the mind—a unique contribution to the genre of devotional literature.

In these pages you will get to know the heart and mind of E. Stanley Jones. Each of these devotionals stands on its own with the following characteristics:

1. You look through a window of insight into the mind of Stanley Jones.
2. You read a life vignette that illustrates a foundational concept that informed his ministry.
3. You discover a pivotal principle that has application to the current context.
4. You "meet Jesus again for the first time." And this Jesus challenges your vested assumptions about what it means to be a Jesus-follower.

Devotion that is more "heat than light" has done immense damage to God's work throughout the ages. Deep devotion rooted in scriptural insights and founded on sound theological principle has invariably been characteristic of the saints through the ages who have done the most to make a lasting contribution to Christ's Church. If Protestants had saints, E. Stanley Jones would be one.

There is so much to like about this book, so it is folly to begin a detailed recitation. Nevertheless, I cannot resist pointing to an underlying 'Jones-ism' that underscores the heart of his teachings: "Falling forward ... into the arms of grace." Look for it!!

E. Stanley Jones would like this book, and I think you will too.

W. Stephen Gunter, PhD
Director of E. Stanley Jones Professorships and Teaching Evangelist,
The Foundation for Evangelism
Advent, 2020

Preface

E. Stanley Jones (1884–1973) was described by a distinguished bishop as the "greatest missionary since Saint Paul." More than an evangelist, he was the author of 27 books, statesman, bishop-elect (who resigned before consecration), founder of Christian ashrams, ecumenical leader, spokesman for peace, racial brotherhood, and social justice, and constant witness for Jesus Christ. He was a confidant of President Franklin D. Roosevelt and consulted with President Truman. Twice nominated for the Nobel Peace Prize, his ministry in India brought him into close contact with that country's leaders including Jawaharlal Nehru, Rabindranath Tagore, and Mahatma Gandhi.

And he was my grandfather.

My grandfather's approach to evangelism in India was to not attack the non-Christian faiths, but to present Christ as the universal Son of Man without the trappings of Western culture. This new approach to evangelism was enthusiastically received. According to Stephen Graham, a Jones biographer, "Jones was one of the most widely known and universally admired Christian missionaries and evangelists of the 20th century." His books sold more than 3.5 million copies and were translated into 30 languages. Even after a severe stroke at the age of 88 robbed him of his speech, Jones managed to dictate his last book, *The Divine Yes*. He died in India on January 25, 1973. Now, nearly 50 years after his death, his books and sermons remain relevant to today's world. You will discover just how contemporary Jones' writings can be as you enjoy *Thirty Days with E. Stanley Jones*, beautifully written by Dr. John E. Harnish.

As a well-known, engaging, and powerful evangelist, Jones preached more than 60,000 sermons in his lifetime. They show a man who was optimistic about humanity's potential and believed the implications of the Kingdom of God were profoundly positive—and realizable. In his goal to redeem the totality of human and social structures, Jones was engaged in finding Jesus in our contemporary world: "Christ is living today, and I find him in places and movements I had never dreamed of and by the quiet sense of his presence Jesus is forcing modification everywhere." He lived in Christ, he reflected Christ and he believed that experience is available to us when we invite Christ to live in us!

Jones felt free to explore and appropriate any good, any truth anywhere, and he included a wide range of these truths in his sermons and books. He moved easily and creatively from the individual to the social, to the economic and embraced the cultural implications of living a life following Jesus.

My grandfather was recognized as an evangelist who did not ask you to leave your intellect at the door. Rather, his messages engage the mind as well as the heart with the deeper and eternal matters for our world, the meaning of discipleship, and the role of the church. In the recently republished *The Christ of the American Road*, he discusses Christianity emerging in American democracy. In 1944, Jones wrote, "In this country the dream of equal opportunity; where privilege and property is widely distributed; the dream of place where class is abolished and where all persons are valued; a place where race and birth are transcended by the fact of common humanity; a place where our gifts and resources are held not for ourselves alone but as instruments of service to the rest of humanity." He believed this laudable possibility had yet to be fully realized and if democracy cannot be extended to all it will be held by none. "Democracy cannot have invisible walls for some and expansive freedoms for others—not if it is to call itself democracy," he wrote in 1944. "Our doctrine of individualism is wreaking havoc on American life. If the individual is an end in himself then that person remains an eternal child, enslaved to their impulses. Such a person can never have self-discipline and a nation built from such people will necessarily be an undisciplined country. And when that happens, our society is headed for disruption and frustrations."

Written almost 90 years ago, his book "Christ and Human Suffering" speaks to our current personal and collective crisis as COVID-19 marches across our world. Jones moves beyond the 'why' questions and explains how we can use our suffering to contribute to transforming ourselves and others. He affirms that God is with us in this pandemic moment as we open our eyes to a world of hurting neighbors and offer our love and connection to a suffering world.

His words brought hope and refreshment to millions of people from every walk of life and I hope that these passages—skillfully chosen by John E. Harnish—do the same for you.

Anne Mathews-Younes, Ed.D., D.Min.
President, E. Stanley Jones Foundation, 2021

Introduction

"He felt obliged to see himself as having responsibility for the whole world, for as he saw it, that is precisely what a Christian is supposed to do."

(Eunice Jones Mathews, E. Stanley Jones' daughter, Stephen Graham, *Ordinary Man, Extraordinary Mission*, page 10)

In 1964, when E. Stanley Jones was 80 years old, *Time Magazine* proclaimed, "Only Billy Graham could rival his international reputation as a Christian leader." Throughout the early and mid-20th century, E. Stanley Jones was one of the best-known Christian voices in the world. He was deeply involved in the birth of the independent nation of India and tried to fend off the war with Japan and the Korean conflict. His book about Gandhi inspired civil rights leaders Dr. Martin Luther King, Jr. and Rev. James Lawson. Lawson spent five years as a missionary in India and credited Jones with his understanding of Gandhi's emphasis on nonviolence.

Scan this QR code with your mobile device or follow the link below to view a short introductory video from the author:
youtu.be/pzUZ6orCD3M

A counselor to presidents and a close friend of Mahatma Gandhi, his influence reached far beyond the U.S. and his adopted homeland of India. His work as a Methodist evangelist carried him to every continent and his 27 books were published in numerous languages. In fact, it is said that Jones' books kept the Methodist Publishing House in business during the Great Depression.

But does a preacher/missionary from the previous century have anything to say to this generation, many of whom were born after Jones died? I would argue, "Yes!" From his life and work, we can hear a word which is as relevant today as it was 75 years ago. In a day when tensions between races and religions are on the rise globally and the message of the Christian faith seems to be either weak or aligned with a political agenda, the voice of a true World Christian needs to be heard once again.

Perhaps most importantly, Jones models a balance which is frequently lacking in the church and world today. Author Henry Garman says, "He was the most famous Christian missionary of the 20th century, but he was also prophetic; foreseeing the future time when Christians would rediscover what Jesus taught of the Kingdom of God and the implementation of it in practical terms." He was able to hold his uncompromising commitment to Jesus Christ side-by-side with an openness to other world religions. He discovered the balance between personal faith and public witness, spiritual piety and social action. He was able to maintain his own integrity even as he made his way through the maze of politicians and public officials. His commitment to racial equality speaks to the burning contemporary issues in the U.S. and his efforts for world peace are as needed as they were during the Second World War.

Of the many things we could learn this remarkable man, I would lift up three themes:

1. *"Jesus is Lord"*

Jones was well known for lifting his hand and raising three fingers, his symbol for "Jesus is Lord." Without apology, he was clear about his message, however, he offered that witness with a sensitivity to diverse cultures and other world religions. In India, he was able to engage Muslims, Hindus and Sikhs as well as non-believers in open conversation and because they sensed his respect for them, they were willing to listen to him. In our contemporary world, the church needs to rediscover that balance between a clarity of faith and openness of heart.

He also discovered new ways of communicating the faith in a non-believing world, using the methods of other religions, as well as secular venues, to spread the Gospel. COVID-19, the technological revolution and the demands of our day call the church to discover new avenues for presenting the faith, an approach which we can learn from Jones.

2. "The Kingdom of God"

Every student of the Gospels knows the primary theme of Jesus' parables was the Kingdom of God, but few rank and file Christians can explain exactly what that means for their daily lives. E. Stanley Jones was captured by a vision of living in the Kingdom and working for the Kingdom. He believed the Kingdom of God held within it what Henry Garman called "a wiser and better radicalism" than other worldviews, particularly communism and greedy capitalism. This led to his life-long commitment to racial equality, world peace and economic justice.

In India in the 1930s, the struggle for independence from British rule was the overriding issue confronting the nation and the church. At the 90th anniversary celebration of the Sat Tal Ashram, Rev. Dr. Naveen Rao, Principal of the Leonard Theological College said, "The issue was what kind of an India it was going to be once the British left. How would people divided on religious lines come together to make one nation? Would it be a Hindu India or would there be a place for Muslims in the new emerging India? For E. Stanley Jones, his missionary task involved that of a statesman, trying to bring two warring sides together."

Writing in 1944, while Japanese Americans were imprisoned in camps and African Americans were suffering under Jim Crow laws, Jones spoke of the vision of equality for all: "Let us go out to stimulate everybody and throw open the doors of equal opportunity to every single person. We must galvanize beaten down people and make them have a faith in God, in themselves and in the future. This would apply to the African American, the Japanese American, the Latino and the Native American. And this faith in humanity would apply to people outside our own borders."

Jones believed living in the Kingdom of God called for a balance between the personal and the social, the pietistic emphasis of the evangelicals and the social engagement of the liberals. He says, "To preach the

Person (of Jesus Christ) without the Kingdom makes religion degenerate into a private affair between you and your personal savior. It lacks social conscience and social redemption. But if you put them together, your religion is at once personal and social. Therefore, I am not interested in a 'personal gospel' or a 'social gospel.' I want one gospel—a gospel which lays its hand on all of life, personal and social, and controls and redeems it. The answer is not Christ, as we often say; the answer is Christ the Person embodying the Order, the Kingdom."

His wife, Mabel Lossing Jones, made an incredible impact in her own right. In addition to his respect for her ministry, Jones clearly affirmed the role of women in his ministry and in the public sphere when he identified equality of women as one of the "great hesitations" of American democracy: "The hesitation to give full equality to women," he writes, "has been long and agonizing. Man will have to give complete equality to women or find the nemesis of history working out as it now seems to be working. Let both men and women be themselves and make their distinct contribution and let women be true to her call and destiny." It was all a part of what it meant to live in the Kingdom of God.

3. *The Ashram Movement and the Roundtable Conference*

These two initiatives represented E. Stanley Jones' practical application of the Kingdom of God at work in human relationships. Growing out of his personal experience at Mahatma Gandhi's ashram, Jones created the Christian ashram. Open to people of all faiths, the only qualification for participation was an openness to the Gospel and a willingness to search for truth with complete honesty. In the ashram, Christians and non-Christians could "live in simplicity in Indian style, wearing Indian clothing, eating simple Indian food, doing menial and manual work with few or no servants. The purpose was to build a model community of the Kingdom of God in touch with the soul of India."

Jones' Ashrams continue today in the work of the United Christian Ashram, but on a broader scale, both the ashram and the roundtable suggest ways of seeking common understanding which could be helpful in our bitterly divided church, nation and world.

This book is not a biography. Stephen Graham (*Ordinary Man Extraordinary Mission: The Life and Work of E. Stanley Jones*) and Robert Tuttle (*In Our Time: The Life and Ministry of E. Stanley Jones*) have already provided us with detailed biographies. Rather, this book is a set of snapshots which reveal insights into the man and his message for today. Each reading includes a prayer taken from one of Jones' devotional books and though some of the language is dated, I have chosen to quote them as they were written.

Reflecting on his conversion as a 17-year-old youth, Jones famously said, "I felt I wanted to put my arms around the whole world … I have spent the rest of my life doing just that." As his daughter remembered, he simply believed this is precisely what every Christian is supposed to do. How we need to hear the voice of this evangelical preacher and social justice prophet from the 20th century in the first half of the 21st century as we seek to put our arms around the world.

I Want What He Has

Evangelist Rev. Robert J. Bateman was preaching a week of revival services at Memorial Methodist Episcopal Church in Baltimore. In the audience, a 17-year-old Eli Stanley Jones was searching for a faith. In his autobiography, Jones would later write:

> Through his rough exterior, I saw there was reality within. He was a converted alcoholic, on fire with God's love. I said to myself, 'I want what he has.' For three days, I sought. During those three days, I went to the altar twice. One of those times, my beloved teacher Miss Nellie Logan, knelt alongside of me and repeated John 3:16 this way: 'For God so loved Stanley Jones, that he gave his only begotten Son, that if Stanley Jones will believe on him he shall not perish, but have everlasting life.'

Today, most Methodist preachers don't give "altar calls"—and in his own ministry, neither did E. Stanley Jones. But in the early to mid-20th century, the tradition of the altar call was familiar. Growing out of the frontier days of the 1800s, when Methodist camp meetings and revivals focused on preaching for repentance and conversion, a "mourner's bench" was often placed to the side of the tent or meeting house. Here, individuals seeking salvation would come to pray and literally mourn for their sins, often doing so with wails and cries of repentance. As Methodist congregations were planted and churches were built, the focus on evangelistic preaching began to impact the architecture of Methodist buildings, which were centered on the pulpit rather than a high altar and the sacrament (as in Episcopal or Roman Catholic traditions). The kneeling rail in front of the pulpit invited people to "come to the altar" for confession, repentance and salvation, often to the strains of hymns of invitation like *Just as I Am* or *I Surrender All.*

During the Billy Graham crusades, the practice morphed into an invitation to "come forward to accept Jesus Christ as your savior." With no kneeling rail in a massive football stadium, responders would walk to the center of the field and be met by a counselor, who would pray for them and send them on their way. Today, the United Methodist liturgy still includes an invitation to "Christian discipleship" at the end of the worship service. In Southern Baptist churches, worship often ends with an invitation to "walk the aisle and join the church." The traditional altar call, which currently resides in some smaller evangelical churches, also continues to exist in traditional Methodist camp meetings, which are still scattered around the country.

As mentioned earlier, few Methodist preachers of today give altar calls—and, in fact, E. Stanley Jones didn't, either. Jones' lectures were often held in public buildings instead of churches, and at the end, he would offer his audience an invitation to stay for conversation built around a question-and-answer format. People often came by the dozens and hundreds to talk, question and reason together, and many of them went home with the same kind of passion for sharing the love of Christ that Jones had experienced as a youth in Baltimore.

E. Stanley Jones spoke of his Baltimore teenage experience in more than one of his books, including his autobiography, *A Song of Ascents*:

> The third night came. Before going to the meeting, I knelt beside my bed and prayed, 'O Jesus, save me tonight.' And he did! A ray of light pierced my darkness. Hope sprang up in my heart. I went to the church and took the front seat. When the evangelist stopped speaking, I was the first one at the altar. I had scarcely bent my knees when heaven broke into my spirit. I was enveloped by assurance, by acceptance,

by reconciliation. I grabbed the man next to me and said, 'I've got it!'

Jones goes on to describe the lifelong impact of that moment:

I see now it was not an it, it was him. I had him—Jesus—and he had me. We had each other. I belonged. As I rose from my knees, I felt I wanted to put my arms around the world and share this with everybody. Little did I dream at that moment that I would spend the rest of my life literally trying to put my arms around the world, but I have. This was the seed moment. The whole of my future was packed in it.

The question for us today is not about the use of traditional liturgical practice or religious traditions. It's not even a matter of whether or not we have had an emotional experience, like Jones did. The question is whether we have come to what he calls the "seed moment"—the time in our lives when we know that "I have him—Jesus—and he has me." For some it will be a dramatic, emotional moment during an altar call, as it was for Jones. For others it will come through intellectual reasoning, as it did for many of Jones' converts. For others still, it will come through the sacraments of the church and the beauty of liturgy. However the experience comes, it is what Jones would call the moment of "conversion"—a concept that would become a major theme of his ministry and life.

And it all began as he listened to a traveling evangelist and said, "I want what he has."

O Spirit of God, I take my littleness and ally it with Thy greatness, my insignificance and ally it with Thy significance, my love and ally it with Thy love. Now I am set to go—anywhere. Amen.

Jones' prayer bench, made from the altar rail at
Memorial Methodist Episcopal Church.

The Power of One

Sometimes, one person makes all the difference.

One person contributes to a chain of events and encounters, all of which result in something much larger than you might have imagined at the time.

When you examine the life of E. Stanley Jones, you will find one little-known person who made that kind of an impact on his young life. Nellie Logan, a public school teacher, taught Stanley Jones' Sunday school class. Rev. Thomas Long, pastor of Memorial Methodist Episcopal Church in Baltimore, wrote to "Miss Nellie" in 1928, saying, "The two boys, Stanley and his brother Howard, came into the Sunday school at the same time their parents joined the church. They came directly under your care and you had much to do with Stanley's religious life."

Miss Nellie was there when the Jones family joined the church, and she was there the night Stanley experienced his conversion, his "seed moment." She prayed with him at the altar of the church and quoted John 3:16 in a way that the 17-year-old boy would never forget. From the time he left Baltimore to attend Asbury College, in 1903, until the mid-1940s, Jones would write hundreds of letters to Miss Nellie. According to biographer Stephen Graham, these letters "… unveil the heart, mind and soul of this fascinating man much more deeply and intimately than his 28 books and hundreds of published articles."

Through a lifetime of mission work that took him to India, the nations of the Pacific, the continents of Africa, Europe and North and South America, Miss Nellie's letters would follow Jones and give him guidance. One simple Sunday school teacher. One person who took an interest in a boy who came her way. One person who made a major impact on the man who would impact the world with his ministry.

It is the power of one.

Another person who contributed to Jones' life in those formative years was J. Waskom Pickett. When Jones went to Asbury College in Wilmore, Ky., and had no place to stay, a friend helped him find lodging with the L.L. Pickett family. The Picketts had about a dozen children at the time and one of them, J. Waskom, became Jones' close friend. Waskom would eventually travel to India as a missionary and become consecrated as the first Methodist missionary bishop in the country where Jones would ultimately spend most of his life. In many ways, Waskom opened the way for Jones in India and, from there, to the world.

It is the power of one.

To dig deeper, it might be noted that the first friend Jones made when he arrived at Asbury College was Virgil I. Darby, a 30-year-old student from Arkansas whom Jones described as very studious and of a life of "quiet hallelujahs." Darby was the one who found the room for Stanley in the Pickett household, which led to his friendship with J. Waskom, who would share his ministry in India.

It is the power of one.

It is doubtful that Miss Nellie, as she knelt to pray with a teenager in a Baltimore church, had any idea that she was planting seeds that would reap a harvest of blessings in thousands of lives around the world. It is doubtful that Virgil Darby knew, when he introduced Jones to the Pickett family and J. Waskom, that he was introducing Jones to the man who would join him in ministry in a distant land they would both come to love. It is doubtful that J. Waskom Pickett realized his friendship with Jones would be the first of many encounters with the man who would become the greatest missionary of his generation: a counselor to presidents, an advocate for peace, and a citizen of the world. Each of these people contributed to the life journey of E. Stanley Jones in a special way, at a special time.

It is the power of one.

Our lives are an intricate weaving of happenstances and high moments, simple encounters and almost-forgotten experiences. We have all been influenced by a multitude of people on our life journey, but if you look closely you will discover that, often, one particular person had a particular influence at a particular time, all of which contributed to what was to follow—and set the direction for what was to come.

It is the power of one person at one time in one life, and it is a power that all of us have to offer others.

O Christ, if I have the little things to do today, help me to do them in a great way with a great spirit. Save me from pettiness lest my great deeds become petty in the process. For how I do a thing makes me in the doing. Help me to be Christian—always. Amen.

E. Stanley Jones as a student at
Asbury College, Wilmore, Ky.

A Forming of Faith and Conscience

Four years before his death, E. Stanley Jones made one last trip to his alma mater, Asbury College, to preach in its chapel. As he spoke, students knew they were listening to a man who had won the hearts of thousands around the globe—and, even after all these years, his voice had not lost its passion or warmth. As a student feeling drawn toward ministry myself, I listened to this aging gentleman and felt my own heart stirred with a passion to put my arms around the world. Now, five decades later, I reread his sermons and am even more appreciative of his thoughtful approach and captivating message.

E. Stanley Jones first attended Asbury College in 1903. The vibrant spiritual environment he found there touched his inner life and inspired his lifelong ministry. It was here that he first sensed his call to missionary service in India. Here, the faith he claimed as a teenager in Baltimore was formed into a lifetime of service. In my own student days, Asbury College was justifiably proud of its famous alum for his worldwide evangelistic work, and when Asbury Theological Seminary opened its School of Missions, it was named for Jones. The B. L. Fisher Library houses the E. Stanley Jones archives.

Though much was made of his evangelistic work, little was said about Jones' passion for racial equality and social justice. As a student at Asbury College in the '60s—in the heat of the Civil Rights movement—I and many of my fellow students were not aware of the fact that, in 1904, Jones was incensed when an African American preacher was scheduled to speak and then had his invitation withdrawn. At that time Jones wrote, to a friend, "the Mason-Dixon line has not been erased in the minds of some. God have mercy." Once, when he preached in the weekly chapel service, Jones declared that desegregation was a God-founded movement and that resistance to the cause of civil rights would hinder the cause of Christ. Dr. David Swartz, historian and professor at Asbury University describes the day: "Tension suffused Hughes Chapel in 1958 as alumnus and missionary E. Stanley Jones addressed a thousand students and faculty members. His indelicate sermon on racial integration shocked may on Asbury College's lily-white campus. He thundered against segregationists, arguing that their resistance was hurting the cause of Christ and democracy. He railed against racism on this crisp October morning. It was a direct challenge to Asbury's establishment, and everyone in the chapel knew it." In 1959, Jones resigned from the board of trustees at Asbury College because of its commitment to segregation.

Decades later, I learned that Jones referred to racism as "spiritual treason against God." At the height of his career, Jones said that if he was unable to return to his beloved India, he would work in America for the cause of racial justice. Martin Luther King, Jr. credited Jones' book on Gandhi as one of the things that inspired him in nonviolence. In speaking of the revolution against racial discrimination, Jones wrote, "In the Southern States it is taking the nonviolent form, thanks in large measure to Dr. Martin Luther King, Jr. I was deeply grateful when he said to me, 'I got my first inkling of the possibility of nonviolent non-cooperation from your book *Gandhi—An Interpretation*, and I determined to apply that method to the doing away of segregation in our land.'"

In the light of the current struggles surrounding racial injustice, Jones' call for racial equality rings as relevant now as it did then. In his 1944 book *The Christ of the American Road*, Jones described his observation of a group of African American students reciting the Pledge of Allegiance. He wrote:

> Seldom have greater words been put together than the words, 'One nation, indivisible, with liberty and justice for all.' (Note: 'under God' had not yet been added to the

pledge.) That is the very essence of democracy. But as these children repeated the word, I said to myself, 'How can they say, "with liberty and justice for all?" They haven't liberty. They are bound by all sorts of restrictions and segregations other people are not bound by, and they certainly do not get justice in our democracy.' Democracy cannot have invisible walls for some and be open for others—not if it is to remain democracy. It cannot have a part of its citizenry able to sing 'My country tis of thee, sweet land of liberty,' and another part unable to sing it because liberty is denied.

Jones spoke forcefully of two Americas: one of freedom, the lover of liberty, and the other pledging, "With liberty and justice for white people." Of the latter, he said, "I do not love that America. It is a false America, a traitorous America and a greater danger to our democracy than Fascism. I want America to be the real America—with liberty and justice for all."

E. Stanley Jones died in 1973. The intervening years have seen significant changes at Asbury College, in the church, and in our nation. Even so, one can't help but wonder what a difference it would have made if we had heeded Jones' call to balance evangelical fervor with social passion and a more robust stand for racial equity. Five decades later, when white supremacy is on the rise and racial bigotry flows on social media with angry rhetoric fueling the fires of division, we need to hear Jones' words:

There is one thing that is troubling our people in America at the present time. We put all kinds of alibis around the central thing—racial egotism. We don't want the blacks to rise because it hurts our pride and we want to be on top. We analyze it here and rationalize it there, but down underneath, the problem is a false belief in the racial superiority of white people.

May the faith and the conscience of this evangelist/prophet, which was formed in his college days, inspire us once again.

O God, who hast made of one blood all men everywhere and hast bound us at Thy feet in brotherhood, help us to get rid of everything that makes for separation between man and man of whatever race or color. For all are equal in Thy sight. Amen.

Note: The audio recording of Jones' 1969 Asbury College sermon can be found at the Asbury University Archives (https://www.asbury.edu/academics/resources/library/archives/).

4

A Log Jam of Wills

As a student at Asbury College, Jones had no notion of being a missionary. In a poem composed for a fellow student who was planning to be a missionary to Argentina, Jones wrote, "But, I said, 'You my brother, heed the call.'" Later, Jones would write, "It never occurred to me that I should heed the call to the mission field."

During his involvement in the student volunteer movement, Jones became burdened by the needs of Africa—even though, in those days, he felt that going to Africa was a very grim proposition—almost like signing one's own death warrant. Even so, as graduation neared, Jones became convinced that that was his direction.

How surprised he was when the president of Asbury College wrote, "It is the will of the faculty, the student body and the townspeople, and we believe the will of God, for you to come and teach at this college." At the same time, a trusted friend was telling Jones that he was convinced it was God's will for him to do evangelistic work in America. Soon after, Jones received a letter from the Methodist Board of Missions, expressing a desire for him to go to India. Jones described it:

> A perfect log jam of wills. I had to have a clear way out.
> Others' interpretation of God's will for me would not do.

> In a time of prayer and reflection, I sensed an inner voice saying, 'It's India.'

What if Jones had gone to Africa instead of India? What if he had accepted the invitation to be a college professor, or an American evangelist? What if he had not gone to Asbury College in the first place? What if, as a teenager in Baltimore, he had not been so intent on seeking out his "seed moment"? What if Nellie Logan hadn't been there to encourage him?

Where was God's will in all of this?

Jones' "log jam of wills" leads us to ask the underlying question: Is God's will something eternally preordained, and if we don't find it, we risk making a major mess of our lives? Or is God's will to be found in the blend of voices and experience, influences and insights, and opportunities and observations that come our way? Is God's will more creative and flexible, working in unexpected ways in order to guide us in our decision-making, to make the best use of our talents and lives? Rather than coming like a steamroller or a thunderbolt, doesn't God's will come more often with all the force of nudge—just a whisper or a hint, pointing us in the direction we should travel?

Jones' final decision was based on a quiet, gentle, inner voice calling him to India, but perhaps it was also a result of all that had come before—all of the people he had encountered, coupled with all of the prayer and reflection of an earnest college student.

Rev. Michael Lindvall, pastor emeritus at The Brick Presbyterian Church in New York City, wrote a wonderful little novel about a young pastor in a small town called *Good News from North Haven*. When his lead character, Pastor David, learns that his call to North Haven was in fact the result of mixed-up letters, it shakes his confidence in believing that he is where God wants him to be. Then, he writes: "I know so much that has come upon me I did not search out and choose, but rather found by chance and accepted as grace. The will of God is the infinitely intriguing weaving of incidents and accidents, plans and providence. Sometimes it works through us, sometimes in spite of us, but in all things it can work for good."

Looking back over his long and productive life, E. Stanley Jones wrote, in his last book: "Fifty years later, I knelt in the same room where I got my first call and said, 'Lord, thank you for telling me 50 years ago it was India.

Give me my life choices to make all over again, and I would make them as I have made them, with this proviso, that where I have been untrue, I would be true."

The record confirms God's blessing and guidance in Jones' life. It was fruitful and fulfilling for him and for the world. In retrospect, it is easy to say, "It must have been God's will." But sometimes, in the moments of decision amidst a log jam of wills, all you have is a quiet inner voice whispering, "It's India"—and you go with it, believing that, in all things, God will work for good.

And in the end, God does.

O God, I come to Thee to be guided, for I know in Thy guidance is my only goodness and my only greatness and my only gladness. So I come to submit my way to Thy way, to align my will to Thy will. I want to know Thy will and to follow it. If Thou hast any word to speak to me this day through the church and through society, let me take that word and follow it. But give me the discernment to hear Thy word amid the words. Guide me. Amen.

John Wesley preaching on his
father's grave in Epworth, England,
"The World is my Parish."

5

Experience and Expression

Though he was clearly a citizen of the world and was regularly welcomed by ecumenical groups and various denominations, E. Stanley Jones was always proud to be identified as a Methodist Christian. In his characteristic way of speaking in simple terms without being simplistic, Jones described his understanding of Methodist tradition in two words: experience and expression. He wrote, "If I were to pick out two of the things the Methodist movement was raised up to emphasize, I would pick out these two—the warmed heart and the world parish—experience and expression."

The experience of the warmed heart

John and Charles Wesley were ordained clergy in the Church of England. In 1736, they were sent as Anglican missionaries to the American Colonies, settling in Savannah and St. Simon's Island, Ga. Given their arrogant, self-righteous stance, they were not well received by the Colonists and were never able to reach the Native Americans. As the story goes, John Wesley fell in love with a woman named Sophie Hopkey—and when she married someone else, he refused to serve her Communion. At this, the Colonial women attacked him; the governor turned against him; and the Wesley brothers fled in despair. Ultimately, this dark journey led John

Wesley to a meeting in Aldersgate Street, in London. On May 24, 1738, he
recorded in his journal:

> In the evening I went unwillingly to a meeting in Aldersgate
> Street where one was reading from Luther's preface to the
> Book of Romans. While he was describing the change God
> works in the heart by faith, I felt my heart strangely warmed.
> I knew that I did trust in Christ for my salvation and an
> assurance was given me that he had taken away my sins,
> even mine, and freed me from the law of sin and death.

John Wesley's so-called "Aldersgate Experience" was the launching
pad for the Wesleyan revival in England and the spread of Methodism
around the world. Since that event, Methodists of many denominations
have claimed the experience of the "warmed heart" as part of their religious heritage. What is now called the Wesleyan Quadrilateral took the
long-established pattern of "Scripture, tradition and reason" and added
"experience," thereby forming the four-way test for truth.

The expression of the world parish

The second theme that Jones emphasized was "world parish." Again,
it comes from the early days of the Wesleyan revival and the ministry of
John Wesley. Like Martin Luther before him, Wesley did not intend to
start a new denomination; rather, his movement was a call for revival
in the dormant body of the Anglican Church. Also like Luther, Wesley's
challenge was not well received by the religious establishment, and he was
banned from preaching in Anglican pulpits. When Wesley returned to
Epworth, where his father had served as rector, he was refused admittance
to the pulpit—so he stood outside, on his father's tomb, to preach to the
gathered crowd. When asked by the bishop to identify his parish, Wesley
famously said, "I look upon the whole world as my parish." Thus began the
missional and evangelistic outreach of Methodists, with the desire to wrap
their arms around the world.

Early American Methodist preachers were called "circuit riders"
because they rode by horseback from congregation to congregation and
from town to town, sometimes covering large sections of geography. They
were commissioned to see their area of responsibility, or their "parish," not

simply in terms of the gatherings of Methodists but as a ministry to an entire geographic area. They were not tied to one pulpit, and they saw the whole world as their parish.

The life of E. Stanley Jones is an exquisite example of this blend of experience and expression, the warmed heart and the world parish. In his quiet, evocative style of preaching, Jones invited his listeners into an engaging experience with the faith and, in his untiring peripatetic travels, he literally covered the world with his ministry. His heart and his wife, Mabel, were in India, but he was constantly on the move because he saw the entire world as his sphere of ministry.

Today, we might expand upon Jones' use of the terms "experience" and "expression" to include the balance between personal faith and social action—the invitation to discover the deep, inner experience of God's grace and then exhibit that in words and actions that address the needs of the world and the issues of the day. For Jones, the experience of the warmed heart moved him into the active, outward expression of the faith, in a desire to put his arms around the world.

And he did.

O blessed Spirit, Thou hast brought into being the way to live corporately. Then help us to yield to Thee so that in us that Fellowship may be realized again. Amen.

6

The Day Democracy Died

E. Stanley Jones' first encounter with racial prejudice came during his youth, in his hometown of Baltimore. He describes it in his autobiography:

> The moment I put my feet upon the Way a new reverence for a person as a person came into my heart. I was in a streetcar with my beloved teacher Miss Nellie Logan. The car was full. When a Negro woman got in and had to stand, I got up from my seat, tipped my hat and gave her mine. A twitter ran through the car. I was giving a seat to a Negro! And I touched my hat in the process! That was over 64 years ago and I had just committed myself as a new Christian to a reverence for people and their possibilities, apart from race, color and status.

Throughout his ministry in India, Jones worked to break down barriers of religion, caste and race. Yet his ongoing concern about racial strife in America never left him. In 1942, Jones was faced with severe criticism from Southern churchmen. Based on his open criticism of the Jim Crow laws, these churchmen tried to block Jones from speaking because, as they believed, he leaned "dangerously toward communism, socialism and especially equality between the races." Jones' response was blunt:

> You say I am guilty of outspoken advocacy of bitter opposition to the Jim Crow laws. If that is a crime, then I plead guilty. If asking for equal rights for citizens of an American democracy is a crime, I plead guilty. It is treason against Democracy and the Christian faith to advocate inequality of treatment of the races.

Jones' first devotional book, *The Way*, was published in 1946. It includes a reading entitled "Reconciling Between Races," which ends with a prayer and an affirmation:

> O God, who has made of one blood all persons everywhere and hast bound us at Thy feet in brotherhood, help us to get rid of everything that makes for separation between persons of whatever race or color. For all are equal in Thy sight. Amen. Today I shall see in every person of every race, not a problem but a possibility.

Seeing every person as a possibility instead of a problem was central to Jones' vision of the kingdom of God at work in human experience. His lectures, ashrams and round tables were unabashedly and intentionally open to men and women of all races, religions, nationalities and backgrounds.

Many conservative evangelicals who loved Jones' passionate witness for the lordship of Christ were offended by his outspoken advocacy for racial equality. In *The Christ of the American Road*, Jones describes a meeting in an unnamed city in the South. It was the primary election day, and African Americans had been summarily disenfranchised with a simple question when they came to register: "Did you vote for the Democratic ticket in 1876?" No one could answer in the affirmative, so they were not allowed to vote. Of course, white voters were not asked the same question. That night, in his meeting, Jones announced, "I have an obituary notice to read: 'Democracy died today in the city of _____ when American citizens were denied the right of suffrage because of the color of their skin. To those who have eyes to see, the ballot box will henceforth be draped in mourning.'" Newspapers reported on this event, with their front pages headlined, "Jones Reads Obituary for Democracy."

The obituary was just one of many times Jones called for the full inclusion of African Americans in society and for breaking down the barriers of race around the world. In another example, when America was heading into the Civil Rights struggle in 1963, Jones wrote:

> I saw in a newspaper a picture of signs which had been taken down and were now in the ash can. They read 'For Whites Only.' We are fast dumping such signs in the ash can. That is where they belong—they belong to a discarded and outgrown past.

Jones' last book, *The Divine Yes*, was dictated in his 88th year following a severe, crippling stroke. Even in the last months of his life, Jones continued to share his passion for racial equality. The following paragraph was dictated while he was in a Cambridge, Mass., nursing home, in April of 1972:

> I am thankful that even as a boy, I came to terms with the race problem. The problem is not race, for clearly a variety of races is the will of God. It is a problem of attitude of those who practice racial prejudice. This is sin. Long ago, I saluted the rising race—the Negros. I am thankful I have lived long enough to see giant strides in resolving and healing the disease of racism in our society. I could wish that I would live to see it entirely wiped out, not only in our own nation, but throughout the lands of the earth. Perhaps that would be the Kingdom of God fully come.

Like Martin Luther King, Jr., E. Stanley Jones did not live long enough to see his vision of a racially inclusive society come to fruition. And regrettably, we are still confronting many of these issues today. When we see overt acts of bigotry and subtle forms of institutional racism still at work in our society, we know that the kingdom of God has not yet fully come. When we see hostility toward Hispanic migrants, the blocking of immigration from predominantly Muslim nations and violent antisemitism directed at Jewish synagogues, we see evidence of our lingering struggle with matters of race, ethnicity and diversity in America.

Dr. David Swartz, historian and the author of *Facing West: American Evangelicals in an Age of World Christianity*, includes a lengthy chapter about Jones and his commitment to racial justice. He reminds us that today we would find Jones' vision of a "color blind" society as outdated and perhaps naïve, but still the voice of E. Stanley Jones calls the church and the nation to confront our collective, deeply embedded original sin and find a way to put our arms around one another and around the world, in order to build a society in which every person of every race is seen not as a problem, but as a possibility—where there truly is liberty and justice for all.

O Spirit of Truth, give me eyes to see a brother in every person, a person for whom Christ died. Take out of my inmost being all lingering prejudices and fears. Let me catch Thy attitudes, and then I shall be free. Amen.

Mabel Lossing, as a college student.

Trailblazing Women

It was the first decade of the 20th century. A young student, on the verge of graduation from Upper Iowa University, found herself in a conversation with a woman from India. The woman was describing the educational needs in India, and she presented to Mabel Lossing a blunt question: "What are your plans for after you graduate?"

"Oh," Lossing replied, "I plan to teach, probably at home."

The woman responded, "Dozens of people here could take your place. Have you ever thought about going to India to teach?"

That was the turning point in Mabel Lossing's life. In 1904, she was commissioned as a missionary teacher and boarded a ship bound for India.

Mabel Lossing was not the first Methodist woman to sense a calling to India. Thirty years earlier, in 1869, two other courageous women—Isabella Thoburn, sister of Bishop James Thoburn, and Clara Swain—built the first women's college and the first hospital for women in Asia. These women opened the way for Indian women to find new opportunities and, ultimately, to live in a new nation: an independent India.

Lossing would follow the path these women forged and end up serving for 42 years, in a country she came to love. There she would meet and marry E. Stanley Jones, give birth to their daughter, and spend her life wrapping her arms around the world. Together, the Joneses' work would impact thousands of lives—but for Mabel, that impact would be seen most deeply in the lives of local female teachers and boys.

In 1912, following their marriage, E. Stanley and Mabel moved to Sitapur to take over the operation of three failing schools. As Stanley was constantly traveling on his preaching missions, the work fell to Mabel. In a biography of Mabel Jones, entitled *A Love Affair with India*, Martha Chamberlain writes, "To attribute to one individual Mabel's full-time profession as educator, administrator, innovator, fund-raiser and nurse to her boys in the boarding school stretches the imagination." Mabel's recently published journal gives a detailed and personal insight into her life and work at the school.

Through two world wars and the Great Depression, Mabel was able to keep the school afloat with her dogged determination and hard labor. Mabel detailed some of her work in a letter to the New York mission office: "I suspect that few missionaries have as much desk work as I have, a boarding school with more than a hundred boys, eight to fifteen medical cases a day, all my husband's mail to attend to (he is never home), a house to look after, a little girl to educate, a farm to run and a dozen interviews a day." All of this in a day before electricity or running water and in a land where the temperature could easily reach 120 degrees.

And she succeeded.

Today, the Mabel Jones Boys School (renamed in her honor in 1961) continues to change the lives of young men who often become leaders in the nation. The work she initiated set the course for education in India for years to come. Her biographer, Martha Chamberlain, writes:

> When Mabel was sent to rescue the school, little did anyone expect that by her sheer work, will and faith she would change elementary education throughout northern India. Through her courageous innovations, not only are women teachers acceptable for boys, but a new respect for women pervades the system. Even today, about a thousand boys continue to be educated each year through Mabel's scholarships.

As evidenced by his support for Mabel, E. Stanley Jones was an advocate for the full inclusion of women in the life of the church, the nation and the world. In his 1944 book *The Christ of the American Road*, Jones identified America's unwillingness to grant women their full place in society as one of the "great hesitations" in the nation. Through his inclusion of women in leadership roles in the ashrams and in his meetings around the world, Jones tried to address this issue.

At the turn of the 20th century, these heroines blazed a trail for women around the world. In the 21st century, with the election of the first woman to serve as vice president, we honor trailblazing women who take their place in leadership in politics, business, Christian ministry and other careers. Isabella Thoburn, Clara Swain and Mabel Lossing Jones changed the lives of countless women, as they sought to put their arms around the world.

Today, we rise up and call them blessed.

O Christ, take my life and bless it and break it and hand it out to others, for I would be free of all inner tied-up conditions. I would be free—to give. Thou hast given me all; help me to give all. Amen.

Mabel Lossing Jones and Stanley
Jones, on their wedding day.

A Need I Had the Power to Meet

In describing E. Stanley Jones and Mabel Lossing Jones, biographer Stephen Graham wrote: "By 1930, Stanley was well known for his Christian evangelism among the intellectual, middle and upper class of India. Less well known was the equally important role of his wife Mabel in educating hundreds of boys who would later assume important Christian and secular leadership roles in Indian society."

In a day when we can travel anywhere in the world in 24 hours, it is hard to remember that, in the early 1900s, the trip to India by ship could take weeks or months. When missionaries were assigned to a foreign post, they would typically stay for 10 years before taking a furlough. For 26-year-old Mabel Lossing, to venture out on her own was a daunting commitment. Of her decision to follow her calling to India, Mabel wrote, "I became a missionary because I was conscious of a need I had the power to meet, and because I felt that if I failed to respond to that need, I could not pretend to be a follower of Jesus Christ."

Mabel's experiment in education was a radical concept in India at the time: a boys' school with women as the teachers. Given the low status accorded to women by Indian society at the time, the first reaction by critics and students alike was a questioning of whether boys could learn from women. In a very short time, however, the school proved to be a great success. Students were drawn from across the spectrum of Indian society.

In 1913, Bishop Frances Wesley Warren wrote, "The experiment has more than exceeded our highest expectation."

At its peak, the school was housing, feeding and training about 130 boys per year—all of whom were supported by Mabel's personal fundraising activity. On top of her administrative responsibilities, Mabel would write an average of 20 letters a day to donors in the U.S., in order to seek the funds necessary to keep the school operating and provide scholarships for the students. In her letters, she shared the many challenges she faced: extreme heat, floods, malaria, dengue fever, and even snakes! Mabel hated snakes.

E. Stanley was constantly traveling and often was away from his wife and daughter for extended periods of time. His longest absence lasted six years, during the world war, when Mabel and their daughter, Eunice, were in India and Stanley was in the U.S. (Stanley was unable to get a visa from the British to return to India, because of his support for Indian independence.) During these times, the full responsibility of the school, of raising their daughter, and caring for the family's financial needs (including Stanley's neglect of his income taxes) fell to Mabel. In one of her letters, she shared her typical day, which would begin at about 6 a.m. and end at 7 p.m. She adds, "An early dinner because I am alone and want to get at a pile of unanswered letters. Then I shall soon climb the stairs, look up at the stars and commit the day to God."

During her time in India, Mabel became a friend of Mahatma Gandhi in her own right and carried on an active correspondence with him, which lasted 25 years. In retirement, she wrote a 358-page textbook on education patterned after Gandhi's model, with an emphasis on peace, nonviolence and truth.

Near the end of her decades in India, Mabel was frank as she shared her frustrations, particularly with the seemingly intractable problems of poverty, caste and the worship of animals. She wrote of an encounter with an Indian official, as she observed the poor and destitute alongside honored and protected cattle:

> Yes, I was tired, but I hope he did not see the resentment that lay under the tiredness. Resentment at the life that spawned and overflowed in spite of dire poverty and overcrowding. Resentment of the mentality that could let lepers and

blind beggars and starving children roam the streets and do nothing about it. The mentality that could accept caste and worship cows and monkeys. Resentment at poverty and suffering. Resentment against the heat, savage and unrelenting with devastating effects on energy and tempers.

At that point, an English doctor and friend told her, bluntly: "Your work in India is finished. You must go home." And she did.

Mabel outlived Stanley by five years and died at her home in Florida in 1978—one month after her 100th birthday. Along with Stanley, Mabel had spent her life putting her arms around the world because she was aware of a need that she had the power to meet.

Mabel Lossing Jones represents a generation of courageous women in the early 20th century who felt called to missionary service—many of whose stories have never been told. At a time when the assumption was that a missionary wife would care for the family and support her husband as he carried out his career, the Joneses were ahead of their time. Like Mabel, who carried on her work in the shadow of a more famous husband, these were women who were conscious of a need they had the power to meet—and they went out to do just that.

O God, open my eyes to see, to see the needs around me. I promise that I will give myself to meet these needs with all I have and am. For I want to be guided into something that takes me and my energies and my love. I will follow—lead Thou me on. In Jesus' name, amen.

The Most Explosive Word in Our Nation's History

More than 75 years ago, E. Stanley Jones wrote:

> When the Declaration of Independence was written these words were used: 'All men are created equal and endowed by their Creator with certain unalienable rights.' When the word 'all' was written into that sentence, little did the authors know it would live to disturb and awaken the soul of this people. The word 'all' was inevitable, for there would not have been democracy if it had been left out, but once it was in, it has become the most explosive and revolutionary word in our nation's history. We have trouble with the word 'all.' We cannot let it go, and we cannot go to it. It will not let us rest until we say the words 'all men' with complete abandon and with no reservations. The history of that word 'all' is the history of the progress of America, and our future progress depends upon what we do with it.

As was typical of his day, Jones used the phrase "all men" in a generic sense. If he were writing today, I am sure he would say "all people." By contrast, we know that when the Founding Fathers said "all men," they didn't mean to include African American men or Native American men, and certainly not women. However, as Jones noted, once the word "all" was in, it became the most explosive and revolutionary word in our nation's history. Almost three centuries following our country's founding, we are still having trouble with the word "all."

In his book addressed to the American church and society, Jones focuses on the use of the word "all" in relation to what he calls "the seven hesitancies of democracy." The list includes labor, race and Americans of Asian origins, as well as the hesitancy to apply the word "all" to women. He writes:

> We have hesitated to apply the word 'all' to women, and yes, it was a woman who started this stream of Christianity and democratic civilization in the West, the first convert in Europe, Lydia, a seller of purple. She certainly started something and yet man has coolly assumed possession of that movement, as if he were the author and finisher of the whole process. If the future belongs to co-operation and women represent the co-operative spirit, then women are to be, in literal fact, the psychic center of power in that future. The hesitation to give full equality to women has been long and agonizing.

It's as simple and as complicated as this: All means all.

Tell me, what part of "all" don't we understand? All means all, regardless of race or place of birth. All means all, regardless of gender or sexual orientation. All means all, in that we believe *all* people are "endowed by their Creator with certain unalienable rights." Until we are able to say "all" with complete abandon and with no reservations, we will never fulfill the Patriots' dream that sees beyond the years.

One of the thrilling things about the incredible musical *Hamilton* is the ability to see the Founding Fathers played by actors of diverse racial and ethnic backgrounds. Even though we know that, historically, all of the Founding Fathers were white males, it is in our current age that people whom we often refer to as "ethnic minorities" are claiming the story as their own—singing to the world that the American story belongs to all of us, and not just some of us.

As Jones relayed, the history of the word "all" is the history of progress in America, and our future progress depends on it. May this explosive, revolutionary word continue to disturb us and awaken us, until we can say with complete abandon and no reservations, "All people are created equal."

O God, when I think of all this, hope springs up within my breast. When we are dreaming of a world of brotherhood, it is not an idle dream—it is a possibility. Amen.

You Mean Jesus Isn't an American or a Brit?

Biographer Stephen Graham describes E. Stanley Jones' first book as something that "burst like a bombshell on Western Christendom." The title of the book was *The Christ of the Indian Road*, and in Jones' gentle but direct way, it challenged the presumptions of Western Christianity. Jones' book invited readers to a new sensitivity to what the message of Christ might mean in the Indian context—even suggesting that Western Christianity had something to learn from India.

"His insight that Christ needed to be freed from identification with Britain and the West met with resistance from fellow missionaries," states author and retired seminary professor Steve Harper. "They were perplexed and caricatured him as having become a modernist."

Jones' book sold widely almost overnight, and it was ultimately translated into 15 languages. Jones followed his first book with a second in 1939, the latter of which expanded on the theme and was entitled *Along the Indian Road*. The image of "the road" showed up in other books, too, such as *The Christ of the American Road* and *The Christ of Every Road*.

In 1925, many citizens of India assumed that Christianity was closely tied to the values of the British Empire or the American experience. As the British Empire expanded around the world, the Colonists did, indeed, see the propagation of Christianity as part of their mission—melded with the spread of the English language, culture and traditions. Biographer Robert

Tuttle concludes that Jones was "one of the first to realize that Western Christianity generally and Western Christian missionaries in particular were consciously or unconsciously often co-opted into becoming agents of Western Imperialism."

As India engaged in the struggle for independence from British rule, the issue became more of a concern for people like E. Stanley Jones. Jones realized that if the Gospel was to take root in the soil of India, it would need to be seen on its own merit and free from the trappings of the British Empire. An American Jesus or a British Jesus simply would not do. So, he constantly sought to present Jesus Christ in ways that would rise above the cultural connection with the West and take root in the life of India.

As author Steve Harper notes:

> All this happened a hundred years ago, but the need to liberate Christ is as great now as it was then. The person of Jesus looks too much like a citizen of America and too little like the Christ. The values of our acculturated Jesus express the values of a capitalist/corporate America more than they express the ethos of simplicity, equity, compassion and generosity. God is always looking for people who will separate the chaff of an acculturated Jesus from the wheat of a universal Christ. He found such a person in E. Stanley Jones. Will he find such persons among us today?

Unfortunately, what we are currently seeing is the rise of "Christian Nationalism" in the United States: wrapping the cross of Christ in the American flag and assuming that Jesus belongs to us. With growing sensitivity to the global nature of the church, we need to see Jesus in the experience of the Middle East and the Far East; in the African nations and the Nordic states; in both North and South America. The Christ of every culture and every nation. In a world of diverse cultures, we need to rediscover the Jesus who is not an American or a Brit, as we seek to put our arms around the world.

O Spirit of God, I thank Thee that Thou hast uncovered the worthwhileness of a person as a person. The future belongs to this. Help us to belong to it. For Thou art sifting the nations on this. Sift us. In Jesus' name, Amen.

Cover of a recent edition of
Jones' book on Gandhi.

In 1964, Bishop James K. and Eunice Mathews met with Dr. Martin Luther King, Jr., during a reception held at Boston University in Dr. King's honor. While on the receiving line, Mrs. Mathews was identified as the daughter of Dr. E. Stanley Jones, a well-known missionary to India and long-time friend of Mahatma Gandhi. Dr. Jones had written a book entitled, "Gandhi, Portrayal of a Friend," which Dr. King had read.

He informed Bishop and Mrs. Mathews that it was Dr. Jones' book which triggered his decision to use Gandhian non-violent methods in the struggle for human rights in the United States.

Gandhi's Word
to Christians

One of the most treasured books in my Jones collection is a signed, first-edition copy of *Mahatma Gandhi: An Interpretation*, published in 1948. My friend John Park found it for $1 at a yard sale. It is autographed, "Your friend and His, E. Stanley Jones." I have no idea who first purchased it and I assume this is how Jones signed all of his books, but it always reminds me of my friend John and his thoughtful gift.

Though there were many influences that led Martin Luther King, Jr. to his understanding of the potential of non-violence as a tool in the Civil Right movement, this little book contributed to that commitment and is now in the MLK Museum in Atlanta. A trip to India and the ministry of E. Stanley Jones was also formative in the ministry of Rev. James Lawson, who shaped the early Civil Rights movement around Gandhi's model of non-violence. He had served as a missionary in India and came to understand the blend of Gandhi and the Gospel of Jesus through Jones and this book.

Fortunately, the book has been republished under the title *Gandhi: Portrait of a Friend* and is still in print. I consider it one of Jones' most important books for today, at a time when narrow religious prejudices threaten to divide our world and India is struggling over the dominance of one religion, versus an openness to all religions. Jones was able to hold in tension his clear, uncompromising, Christ-centered faith while keeping a deep appreciation for other religions, as he sought to discover a truly Indian expression of the Christian faith. Today, the vision he held for a multi-religious community is needed in America as well as in India.

Twenty-three years before the release of the Gandhi book, Jones spoke of his relationship with Gandhi in *The Christ of the Indian Road*, his first book. Published in 1925, *The Christ of the Indian Road* includes one of Jones' most famous passages, which he repeated in numerous places. In conversation with Gandhi, Jones shared his desire for Christianity to be "naturalized" in India so that it was no longer seen as foreign or connected with Colonialism and Western nations. He asked Gandhi, "What would you suggest we do to make that possible?" The answer is often referred to as Gandhi's advice to Christians:

1. All of you Christians begin to live more like Jesus.
2. Practice your religion without adulterating or toning it down.
3. Put your emphasis on love, for love is the center and soul of Christianity.
4. Study the non-Christian religions and cultures more sympathetically, in order to find the good that is in them, so that you might have a more sympathetic approach to the people.

Jones, in turn, concluded the following:

> The greatest living non-Christian in the world asks us to take the Gospel in its rugged simplicity and high demand. Instead, we have been inoculating the world with a mild form of Christianity, so that it is now practically immune to the real thing. Here is the epitome of the whole thing: From every side India is saying we must be Christian, but Christian in a bigger, broader way than we have hitherto been.

Rev. Naveen Rao, principal of Leonard Theological College in Jabalpur, India, comments on the relationship between Gandhi, Jones and Christianity:

> Gandhi won the heart of Christians by asking them to become better or real Christians as per our own proclaimed faith and its ethics embodied in Jesus Christ. Gandhi did not engage Jones in a debate, rather he helped Jones set his focus on the goodness of the Gospel rather than on the weaknesses of other religions. As a Christian missionary who had gone out to win Indians for Christ, how could Jones not love such a person who turned the focus on Jesus Christ?

From the late 1800s until the Great Depression, foreign missions reached one of its high points in church history. According to Robert Tuttle's *In Our Time*, church agencies spent approximately $60 million on foreign missions in 1928 alone—a staggering amount in those days. This great era of missionary expansion was truly inspired, and it planted seeds that are still bearing fruit today. Yet all too often, missionaries were so closely tied to Western culture (in India, the British Empire) that they failed to develop a truly naturalized Christianity. Sometimes, even today, our missional outreach can be patronizing and paternalistic when we confuse what it means to be Christian with what it means to be American.

A recent book, written by a group of E. Stanley Jones professors at United Methodist seminaries, brings this conversation up to date. *E. Stanley Jones and Sharing the Good News in a Pluralistic Society* includes this summary from Jones' ministry, which would be a helpful model for us today:

> Jones was comfortable engaging those who thought and believed differently than he did. For Jones, engaging the other as a child of God means all individuals must be taken seriously, even when they are very different from us. The ideals of being engaging, dialogical, and relational are foundations to how Jones was able to contextualize the Gospel in a pluralistic society.

Regrettably, it seems there are no photos of Jones and Gandhi together, but if we could hold in our mind's eye the image of Jones and Gandhi sitting quietly in an ashram, sharing their lives and stories, it might change our approach as we seek to put our arms around the world today.

O God, we thank Thee that Thou art leading Thy children everywhere to a union that will not wipe out our differences, but will provide that they exist in a deep and fundamental union. Thou art teaching us. Help us to learn. In Jesus' name, amen.

Gandhi:
Living in the Tension

I am ashamed to confess that a matter of rupees kept me from being present at the greatest tragedy since the Son of God died on the cross.

—E. Stanley Jones

E. Stanley Jones arrived in Delhi 75 minutes before the assassination.

He had requested a time to meet with Mahatma Gandhi, but as his train was five hours late, he and his friend instead planned to attend the prayer meeting Gandhi held each day, hoping for a chance to speak with him then. Jones says they would have had time to make it if they had taken a taxi, but he figured it was too expensive—and so, they would try another day. Expense had decided the matter, Jones later said—otherwise, he would have been present when an assassin took the life of a great man and personal friend.

The book Jones wrote about Gandhi following his death took on major importance in America when it was discovered that Martin Luther King, Jr. had read it and marked in the margin, "This is it." Jones' book and Gandhi's commitment to nonviolent resistance inspired King's activity in confronting the evil of racism in society. In a similar way, the great African American theologian Howard Thurman was impacted by his relationship with both Gandhi and Jones during a life-changing trip to India. In his autobiography, *With Head and Heart,* Thurman reflects on his time with the two men as one of the formative experiences of his life. He dedicated an entire chapter of his autobiography to that experience, titling it "Crossing the Great Divide—India."

Jones himself described Gandhi as "a combination, a meeting place of currents, a holding together of antitheses that seem at first to be in conflict, but in Gandhi, proved to be his strength."

He was a combination of East and West.

The soul of Gandhi was intensely Eastern, but he was formed by the time he spent in the West, studying law in Great Britain and working in South Africa. He spent 26 years outside of India and returned with a global conscience, which informed all he did.

He was an urban man who came to identify himself with the peasant.

Gandhi's upbringing was upper-class, but he put away the trappings of power and wore only what the peasants wore: a simple *dhoti*, or loincloth. He fully identified with the masses, speaking their language and sharing their life, yet never lost sight of what he knew about the seats of power and avenues of influence in the world. He was a living blend of the urban and the rural.

In him, there was a coming together of the militant and the passive.

Jones describes Gandhi as militantly passive and passively militant. For him, passive did not mean weak; rather, it goes back to the original meaning of the word: to suffer quietly and patiently. It was an active resistance of a higher level. This was part of the lesson that Martin Luther King, Jr. took from Gandhi, and what he instilled in the movement for racial justice in America.

The Mahatma combined the mystical and the practical.

Gandhi would arise every morning at 4 a.m. for his devotions, but his mysticism was intensely practical. The best example of this was when he would carry on his religious practices while spinning at his spinning wheel. This would become a symbol for Gandhi's identification with the working class and, ultimately, the new nation of India.

He was a Hindu who was deeply Christian.

Jones acknowledges that Gandhi was Hindu, and yet he believed Gandhi was more Christianized than many Christians. This fascinating combination earned respect from both Hindus and Christians, and it enabled Gandhi to speak with authority to both groups. Jones concludes,

"He was a man in whom opposing virtues and interests were held in a living tension and reconciliation."

Rev. Naveen Rao, principal at Leonard Theological College in India, states the following on E. Stanley Jones and Mahatma Gandhi:

> Jones and Gandhi are the twin brothers, two sides of the same coin. What Jones believed and held central to his faith in the Person of Jesus Christ and in the Kingdom of God, Gandhi was practising even without acknowledging faith in the Person of Jesus Christ and the Kingdom of God. While Jones was holding the faith, Gandhi was doing the exact same thing in his life and work in concrete historical terms.

For Jones, the debate between America's fundamentalists and modernists during the '40s and '50s offered the same challenge of "living in the tension." He believed that if the church focused on Jesus Christ as the absolute, and the kingdom of God as its model, these competing strands of thought could be brought together. He stated:

> The Church has failed to bring to a living synthesis differing emphases within itself. Take the fundamentalist and modernist split—for it is a real split, a rift going straight through American Christianity. If the Church had a real grip on the absolute Person embodying the absolute Order, it would have been able to see that both fundamentalism and modernism belong in the Kingdom of God and that both emphases are necessary.

Learning to live with conflicting values and competing ideas is a challenge for many of us. It is easier to be scholeric and dogmatic, avoiding the inconvenience of contrasting realities. Perhaps that is the appeal of the various fundamentalist movements in the world today, be they religious or political, Muslim or Christian, right-wing or left-wing. But the person who seeks to be fully alive and in touch with the real world needs to be able to find the strength that comes from living in the tension: of holding together what sometimes seems to be opposing virtues in a desire to find reconciliation. To use Jones' language, living in the tension begins with clear commitment to "the unchanging person and the unshakable kingdom," coupled with an openness to the diverse voices at work in the world.

O God, I thank Thee that Thou hast made us of one blood but of many cultures and languages. We are one amidst our differences. Help us to be tolerant of differences and yet one among them. Amen.

Note: Martin Luther King, Jr.'s copy of *Gandhi: Portrayal of a Friend* is on display at the King Center in Atlanta, Ga.

God's Trump Card: Atom or Atma?

Near the end of his book on Gandhi, Jones quotes Napoleon. At the pinnacle of his military success, Napoleon said, "There are only two powers in the world—the power of the sword and the power of the spirit. In the long run, the sword will always be conquered by the spirit." So Jones borrowed that imagery. He used a familiar Indian word, *atma*, to describe the power of the spirit, and contrasted it with "atom," and all it represented at the time. He writes:

> So Mahatma Gandhi is God's appeal to this age—an age drifting toward its doom. If the atomic bomb was militarism's trump card, thrown down on the table of human events, then Mahatma Gandhi is God's trump card which he throws down on the table of events now—a table trembling with destiny. God is appealing mightily to this age through the strange little man, as he has appealed agelessly through The Man, and here the strange little man and The Man are saying the same thing: 'Would that even today you knew the things that make for peace.' The things that make for peace do not lie in the atom and its control for military ends. They lie in the *atma*, and its power to control the atom for the ends of a new humanity for everybody.

The year was 1948. The devastation of the second world war—and, particularly, the incredible destruction of Hiroshima and Nagasaki by the atom bomb, just three years earlier—must have been vivid in Jones' mind as he contrasted these two concepts. He noted:

> We have seen the power of the atom in Hiroshima and Nagasaki, where it left piles of rubble and we have seen the power of *atma* in Mahatma Gandhi where it freed one fifth of the human race and afterwards healed their divisions and gave new hope to a confused and baffled humanity. We have seen both. The issue, then, is atom versus *atma*.

In reflecting on Jones' view of Gandhi as God's trump card, Rev. Naveen Rao states:

> Jones has rightly described Gandhi as the 'Irregular channels' through which God is working on the human scene. A most significant thing is the interpretation of Gandhi by Jones as God's trump, God's channel, God's instrument. It is the most powerful expression of humility, love, acceptance and decoding of a person of different faith, different nationality, and different ideology. Jones' interpretation of Gandhi is the most remarkable and powerful testimony of God's working in our times in the world beyond the church.

If Gandhi was, indeed, God's trump card—played on the table of human events, in the 1940s—what card will we play now, when it is our turn at the table—a table that is still trembling with destiny?

Atma or atom?

O Thou who art gathering up the ages, gather us up and make us one, one in spite of difference, perhaps because of difference. For in Thee all things cohere. Hold us together in a coherent whole. Amen.

E. Stanley Jones with his symbol for
'Jesus is Lord,' at an ashram in Finland.

Life Reduced to Simplicity

"My faith," Jones wrote, in his autobiography, "has been reduced to simplicity: Jesus is Lord. My life answer has been found. I have an answer which is the Answer, and it works. The universe and life approve it—Jesus is Lord."

One of the characteristics of Jones' teaching, preaching and writing was the gift of simplicity. Many of his books are drawn from his day-to-day experiences, including encounters and conversations with the multitude of people he met. He did not consider himself a great theologian but instead saw his calling as an evangelist, sharing the message of Jesus Christ as the core of the Christian faith in a variety of ways and in a variety of cultures, in order to connect with his listeners. The message was simple, but the implications—from racial reconciliation to world peace—were immense.

Wherever he went, Jones would raise his three fingers as a simple sign of greeting, or benediction, to say, "Jesus is Lord." It became the symbol of his message in every language and nation.

Rev. Lynn DeMoss, a retired Michigan pastor, served as a missionary in what was then the Belgian Congo in the late 1950s. DeMoss remembers Jones arriving in Lulumbishi to preach. The crowd waiting for him was so large they were unable to meet inside, so Jones stood on top of a shed behind the church, with the people spread out in the open field. He lifted his hand and called out, "*Yesu ni Bwana!*"—and everyone responded with a raised hand, shouting, "*Yesu ni Bwana!*" Part of the significance was that, until that time, Africans tended to call the white missionaries *bwana*, which means "master." But from that time on, *bwana* referred to Jesus as the only "master."

"And still today," DeMoss says, "when Africans gather to worship, they will call and respond, '*Yesu ni Bwana*, Jesus is Lord.'"

Also serving as a missionary in Congo at that time was diaconal minister and author Betty Cloyd. Recalls Cloyd, "We would see Congolese Christians along the road and they would greet us this way. They are still doing it today."

One of Jones' last books brought together his two favorite themes: the lordship of Jesus Christ and the kingdom of God. Published in 1972, just a year before his crippling stroke, it is entitled *The Unshakable Kingdom and the Unchanging Person*. In the introduction, Jones seems to realize that his time is running short when he states, "As a possible last fling, I'd like to fling my blazing torch of the Unshakable Kingdom and the Unchanging Person amid the burned out heap of extinguished or dying enthusiasms, to set them ablaze again with the relevant—the really relevant, the fact of the Kingdom of God on earth exemplified in Jesus."

Throughout Jones' ministry, the message of the Gospel was wrapped up in those two intertwined images. Jones believed what he called "The Way" is the most natural way for humankind to live.

"When we say that Jesus and the Kingdom are 'The Way,' we don't merely mean they are the way to get to heaven," Jones wrote. "The Kingdom and Jesus are The Way unqualified, the Way to think, to act, to feel, to be—in every relation, in the individual and the collective, for God and man."

Jones' final book, published after his death, comes from the notes he scribbled and the tapes he dictated following his stroke. Some of them were almost incomprehensible, but his daughter, Eunice Jones Mathews, compiled them as her father's last will and testament. The book is entitled *The Divine Yes* and is based on biblical text from II Corinthians Jones frequently used in his preaching: "The divine 'yes' has at last sounded in Him, for in Him is the 'yes' that affirms all the promises of God."

From the day when, as a teenager, he knelt at a church altar in Baltimore, and until his dying day, E. Stanley Jones believed Jesus was the great "yes": the divine "yes" who fulfilled all the promises of God. Jones' legacy to the world in this new century is the kingdom of God and witness to Jesus Christ: the "unshakable kingdom" and the "unchanging person."

For him, it was that simple.

O Christ, how can I ever cease to thank Thee that amid the stumblings of life I happened on this—The Way! It fills me with constant surprise that I, even I have found The Way. My doubts are at rest. Now forward—forever! Amen.

Cardioversion Conversion

My cardiologist said, "You need a cardioversion."

I was dealing with an irregular heartbeat, so the first step was to try to get my heart back into its proper rhythm—hence, cardioversion.

E. Stanley Jones would understand.

One of Jones' primary themes highlighted the need for "conversion," or the need for the heart to be in proper rhythm with the universe and with God. In fact, he wrote an entire book on the subject—and he titled it, simply, *Conversion*. Jones defines conversion as "a change in character and life followed by an outer change or allegiance corresponding to that inner change." That is, life in its proper rhythm begins with the heart—cardioversion conversion.

Jones viewed conversion as "the law of life. Everything" he said, "is under a process of conversion." Jones uses things like photosynthesis, and the body turning food into energy and energy into life's actions, as examples of the process at work in the natural order. Yet clearly, he was talking about something deeper—something more profound than just the normal processes of the universe or the human body. His concern was the conversion of the heart, the mind and the soul, which then results in a life more in rhythm with God's design for human experience.

Once again, Jones relates the story of his own faith experience, his moment of conversion as a teenager in Baltimore—but he adds a personal anecdote showcasing his sense of humor as well as his insight. Following that experience, he says, "Soon the whole community heard about it. Some of my chums who had shared the old life with me couldn't believe it. They said, 'Stanley, you ain't really converted, are you?' My reply was, 'The h— I ain't!' I used the old language to express the new found joy."

Conversion is, Jones noted, "life impinging on life, awakening it, unifying it, setting it aglow, moralizing it, making it care, putting a new zest into everything and making it love." In other words, it is aligning our lives with the purposes of the kingdom of God and discovering an abundant life.

In many of his books, Jones used the image of "The Way" as the pattern for following the life and teachings of Jesus Christ. He believed that "The Way" was written into the life of the universe and that, when we live in accordance with it, we are living in proper rhythm with our bodies, our minds, other persons and the whole of life. He states, "The Kingdom of God and The Way are synonymous because the Kingdom of God is The Way. There are just two things: The Way and not-The-Way. The Kingdom of God is always The Way."

So, he asks his readers:

> Then what is the Christian answer? It is pointed and plain—surrender yourself to God. Self-realization comes through self-surrender. Conversion is conversion from a self-centered life to a God-centered life. Surrender is the best word I know to express what Luther called 'the Joyful Exchange'—the joyful exchange of an egocentric, impossible self for a God-centered, possible self. It is a happy yielding of yourself to God.

I have quoted at length from Jones' book, *Conversion*, because the theme is so central to his life and work. For him, conversion meant cardioversion—getting the heart into its proper rhythm, then living the new life in light of the kingdom of God. "The Way."

All of life depends on it.

O Christ, Thou hast shown me how to live. Help me to live Thy Way, so that I may truly live. I would abound and not drag leaden feet to dead tasks. I would know what it is to be purged of all self-centeredness and to be free to give myself to others. Amen.

E. Stanley Jones at Sat Tal Ashram.

The Ashram: 'Unreservedly, Unbreakably'

Of all the notes that make up my Song of Ascents, one of the most important is the Ashram note. Without it I would have lacked a disciplined fellowship. I would have been a lone wolf howling at the pack about what they should do.

—E. Stanley Jones

Some scholars suggest that the creation of the Christian ashram was E. Stanley Jones' most valuable and lasting contribution to the life of the church in the world. It grew out of his experience at Gandhi's ashram, in the Hindu tradition, and it also reflects an historic practice of the church: the practice of gathering in small groups, beginning with Jesus' original disciples—12 men who came together as his inner circle. The Bible relays Jesus' band of followers soon expanded to include a broad grouping of women and men who were seeking to learn from Jesus together.

In a similar way, Methodist founder John Wesley organized his society with what he called "class meetings" and "bands," which were built around the central question, "How is it with your soul?" In these small groups, early Methodists nurtured their faith and kept each other accountable for their Christian discipline. The "Love Feast" became the celebration of their life together.

In 1930, Jones invited Ethel Turner and Rev. Yunus Sinha to join him in establishing a Christian ashram. They came into possession of a 350-acre estate at Sat Tal (Seven Lakes), in the foothills of the Himalayas. The estate included 18 cottages, clustered around a lake. The purchase price was paid primarily through the sale of Jones' books, and the property was deeded to the Methodist Church of Southern Asia. Emblematic of the future of the ashram movement, the first gathering included both men and women of three nationalities—British, Indian and American. Jones writes, "We hadn't the slightest idea we were beginning something that would become a world movement. We went out like Abraham, not knowing whither we were going."

Whether these founders fully realized it or not, the Christian ashram would become a model community for a nation on the verge of independence. According to Rev. Naveen Rao:

> During this time, the ashram movement was catching on as several leaders involved in the freedom struggle of India were opening ashrams. Ashram became a site of experimenting of what kind of new nation India would like to become once independence was achieved from the British empire. E. Stanley Jones contributed his bit into the pot-boiler with an ashram based on the person of Jesus Christ and in the Kingdom of God. Sat Tal Ashram proclaimed the vision of the Kingdom of God for a new India, which was lived and practiced in a miniature form. It became a model for an emerging nation looking forward to rising above the Caste system and religious, regional, ethnic and linguistic lines to form a loving, sharing and caring community, as exhibited by the early Christians in the Book of Acts.

One clear distinction from the Hindu ashram was the role of the *guru*, the leader. In Gandhi's ashram, he was clearly the *guru* and the program focused on his teaching and personality. In the Christian ashram, Jesus Christ is the *guru* and everyone gathers around the person and teachings of Christ. "Brother Stanley," as E. Stanley became known, was not the *guru* but simply another member of the community. A Hindu who attended an early Christian ashram said, "I expected to see the ashram revolving around Brother Stanley as a *guru*, but to my surprise, Brother Stanley sat with the rest of us, with Christ at the center."

The Christian ashram begins with the "morning of the open heart" and concludes with the "hour of the overflowing heart." The schedule includes time for individual silence and physical work, as well as time for gathered prayer and personal reflection. As the movement made its way to the U.S., Jones' solid commitment to the inclusion of all persons—regardless of race or gender—was a radical and contested stance, particularly in the American South. Yet Jones was insistent that all persons were welcome. The movement has since spread around the world, with Christian ashrams in many nations that reflect the globally inclusive body of Christ.

Jones, during the work hour at an ashram.

As the author of this book, I am writing this chapter during the time of the COVID-19 virus pandemic, when churches have had to cancel corporeal worship and move to online technology for small groups as well as Sunday worship. Though it has forced the church to discover new ways of creatively using technology in ministry, it has also driven home the utter necessity of life shared with other human beings. We are social beings who depend on our relationships with others to provide meaning in our lives. Particularly for Christians, the faith is built around a table with broken bread and a shared cup, where we are all one body. Without this, our lives can become narrow and selfish. Coming out of the COVID year, we have realized our deep need for the fellowship in worship, the encouragement and the accountability that comes from living in community.

At Sat Tal—which is still in use today—all participants stand together as they repeat the motto on the wall: "Unreservedly given to God, unbreakably given to each other." The Christian ashram offers a model for communities in which people gather in the name of Christ, literally putting their arms around each other and, with that gesture, around the world.

O Holy Spirit, quicken our common loyalty to the Kingdom and quicken our life in the Spirit so that we may have an unbreakable unity with those who compete in the same field. Amen.

For further information on the ashram movement today, go to www. christianashramint.org.

ASBURY COLLEGE

HERE WE ENTER A FELLOWSHIP:
SOMETIMES WE WILL AGREE TO DIFFER:
ALWAYS WE WILL RESOLVE TO LOVE,
AND UNITE TO SERVE.

E. STANLEY JONES

17

'Here We Enter
a Fellowship'

E. Stanley Jones' alma mater, Asbury College (now a university), has a long history in the Methodist movement. Founded by a Methodist preacher with the mission of training young men and women in the faith and general education, Asbury has produced generations of preachers and missionaries, as well as teachers, doctors and professionals in every field who live out their faith as they put their arms around the world in service. That was certainly true when E. Stanley Jones was there in 1903, and it was true when I was there in the 1960s.

As a student, I remember walking past a brass plaque in Hughes Auditorium, engraved with a quotation from E. Stanley Jones. This quotation impressed me while I was a student and it continued to impress me through the years of my ministry. I used it in more than one sermon and in more than one church, as a vision for the congregation. Recently I discovered that it was not originally spoken about Asbury College, but rather, it was one of the mottos at Jones' original ashram in India. According to Jones, "The spirit of the Christian Ashram may be gathered from the mottoes on the wall of our meeting rooms: 'Leave behind all race and class distinctions ye who enter here.' We felt the kingdom of God is race- and class-blind, so must our society be."

Another motto:

Here we enter a fellowship;

Sometimes we will agree to differ;

Always we will resolve to love and unite to serve.

For Jones, this was a vision not only for the Christian ashram but also for the church and the global community. He pursued this vision in his work with the Crusade for a Federal Union of Churches, with the creation of the round table conferences, and in his engagement with diverse groups around the world. Evidently, someone at some point in the history of Asbury College thought it was an appropriate vision for the college, and had it engraved on a brass plaque.

The irony is that even as I walked past that plaque, Asbury College was going through incredible internal turmoil. The college had employed four different presidents in four years, and as a campus community, we were *not* able to agree to differ and we were *not* always united in love and service. Fortunately, by the time I was a senior, the campus was coming back together and moving closer to the vision Jones described.

Also during my senior year at Asbury, E. Stanley Jones came back to preach one more time before his death. I don't remember much of the sermon, but I do remember him saying, "Everyone who belongs to Christ belongs to everyone who belongs to Christ." Jones acknowledged that, when he preached around the world, that phrase was always difficult for his interpreters to translate. This vision is not only hard to translate—it is hard to live out, too. Yet it is one more of his sayings that lifts up the importance of the Christian community and the commitment of its members to one another—a motto that still offers a word of hope for the global church and the global community.

As I write, the denomination that nurtured both Jones and myself—the United Methodist Church—is demonstrating the tragic evidence of our inability to agree to differ, to resolve to love and to unite to serve. At the same time, the political polarization in our nation is only too evident. In the church, in our national politics, in our local communities and in our broken world, we need to reclaim the vision of the ashram—the notion of a shared commitment to our brother-sisterhood, in which we can at times agree to differ but still maintain the commitment to love and the desire to serve all humankind, with a passion to put our arms around each other and the world.

O Christ, we know that those who belong to Thee belong to one another automatically and inescapably. Help us to recognize, rejoice in and act on that unity. Amen.

Jones at Sat Tal Ashram with Sister Lia, a Greek Orthodox nun, offering his symbol for 'Jesus is Lord'.

18

The Legacy of the Christian Ashram Today

While a staff member at The Upper Room, Rev. Tom Albin was the executive director of United Christian Ashrams and is well-acquainted with E. Stanley Jones and the Christian ashram movement. His position has given him an in-depth look at the life and work of Jones.

"I really believe," said Albin, "that the preaching and teaching of E. Stanley Jones is as relevant today as it was 70 years ago, and maybe even more so."

Albin continues:

> He was an evangelical, a modernist, a centrist and a
> progressive, all at the same time. He was too conservative for
> the liberals and too liberal for the conservatives. The lessons
> he learned in the multi-religious context of India are still
> relevant in our multi-religious context. In fact, I think we
> need his wisdom, humility and integrity more today than
> they did in the mid-20th century.

Albin believes the unique approach of the Christian ashram is still vital because it offers "… an open-handed invitation to come and see Jesus" (John 1: 39-50). As opposed to heavy-handed evangelism, which demands that a person "make a decision" immediately in order to escape an eternity of torment in hell, the Christian ashram invites persons of all faiths and of no faith to live in community, to share personal spiritual practices and to raise spiritual questions and concerns.

The aim of the Christian ashram is to provide a safe place where individuals can talk about their own journey of faith in the reality of their own context. It is a lived experience of the kingdom of God in miniature, where barriers of race, religion and gender are taken down. There is no use of professional titles like "doctor," "reverend," "pastor" or "bishop." Everyone at a Christian ashram is addressed by his or her first name—for example, "Brother Tom" or "Sister Mary," following the example of "Brother Stanley" Jones.

As these barriers are removed, each person is seen as created by God with a unique fingerprint and a unique perspective on the divine. Therefore, everyone is a teacher and everyone is taught. No one person is higher or better than another. In order to demonstrate this, everyone attending a Christian ashram is expected to do some form of physical work, thereby serving the entire community, or the retreat center where the event takes place. Jones himself delighted in cleaning the toilets, in sharp contrast to the predominant caste system of the Hindu majority in India and in direct continuity with Jesus' own example of service in washing his disciples' feet (John 13:1-16).

Regarding the Christian ashram, Rev. Albin, or "Brother Tom," remarked:

> The Christian Ashram culture of mutuality and respect is not the same as a shallow, modernist approach which often denies the real differences between different faith traditions in order to be nice. Jones believed that Jesus Christ should be the one important topic of conversation. Hindus admire Jesus, Muslims admire Jesus, people of all faith traditions and people with no faith tradition still find Jesus interesting. Brother Stanley affirmed Jesus as the central focus because he believed that Jesus Christ is Christianity and Jesus is Lord.

Albin noted how rare it was for a movement begun by a gifted Christian leader to continue for many years after his/her death. Yet many years after its inception, the Christian ashram movement is alive and growing. This movement is celebrating its 90th year in India and its 80th anniversary in

North America. Recently, new Christian ashrams have been established in the U.S. and in India, on college campuses and in retirement communities. "It is clear to me that God is at work in and through the Christian Ashram movement today and I would invite anyone reading this book to visit our website and 'come and see' for yourself."

O Holy Spirit, indwell us by Thy power and life, so that we may have a sense of togetherness—a sense that when one is hurt, all are hurt, and that when one rejoices, all rejoice. Give us a sense of a Body. Amen.

Note: For more information on the ashram movement, visit the website for United Christian Ashrams: ChristianAshramint.org.

Knights at the Round Table

In the fanciful world of Camelot, the vision of the knights gathered at the round table inspired King Arthur with hope for peace in the world. Unfortunately, jealousy breached the walls of the castle and shattered the round table and the hope it represented. For E. Stanley Jones, however, the round table was not just a fantastic hope; he envisioned it as a present reality and he modeled it in his round table conferences.

Growing out of his openness to insights from the other religions in India, Jones sought a way to bring Christians and non-Christians together. In *Christ at the Round Table*, Jones writes:

> The purpose was to face the question of how religion was working, what it was doing for us and how we could find deeper reality. The valuable thing for us, as Christians in the Round Table Conferences with non-Christians, lay in the fact that we were compelled to rethink our problems in the light of non-Christian faith and in the light of the religious experience of non-Christians.

Jones' public events always ended with a time of question-and-answer, an invitation to conversation—but often, these events drew hundreds of people and did not give the opportunity for in-depth discussion or intimate sharing. In response to that need, Jones created the round table conference, an event during which Christians and non-Christians could sit down together and talk in peaceful terms. At these events, Jones said, "… no one would argue, no one would try to make a case, no one would talk abstractly, and no one would merely discuss religion, but we simply shared what religion is meaning to us as experience."

Whereas the ashrams were designed to bring Christians and non-Christians together in a smaller community over an extended period of time, the round table conference drew community leaders who would invite 40 potential participants, with the goal of getting approximately 30 attendees. Two-thirds of the invitees were intentionally non-Christians, "… so that the non-Christians will not think the Christians have packed the meeting," said Jones. The questions they were asked were not abstract theology, but things like, "What has become real to you?" and "Tell us what you have found through your faith. What does it do for you in your everyday life?" Jones discovered that, in opposition to the West—where individuals tend to avoid talking about religious life—in India, discussing this subject is as natural as breathing, and many individuals were eager for the opportunity. Of course, the round table conference also provided the Christians with the opportunity to share what their faith in Jesus Christ meant in their lives, which often resulted in people coming to faith in Christ.

Beyond the religious context, Jones held out hope that the model of the round table conference could even be used to bring together the nations of the world. He comments:

> Suppose the nations should sit at a Round Table Conference and through their representatives lay before each other what religion was doing for them in experience. Suppose they should tell of what it is meaning for them in their working program, as a dynamic for cleansing the social and economic life, the curbing of selfishness toward others and the creation of the spirit of brotherhood and goodwill for all. What would that national witness be? What would the nations that profess the Christian faith say to the non-Christian nations, and vice versa?

King Arthur's dream for the knights of the round table ended in disarray, and though E. Stanley Jones' global dream was never fully realized, you can't help but ask: "Suppose it did? Suppose *we* did?"

Gracious Father, Thou hast written the family spirit into our relationships with the rest of the Family. When we break those laws we turn the Family into a feud, snarling up our relationships—and ourselves. Forgive us and help us to catch Thy mind in our relationships with other minds, Thy spirit in relation to other spirits. In Jesus' name, amen.

Christians, Unite!

In the late 1930s, the world was in turmoil. The lingering effects of the Great Depression still ravaged the world, the decay of colonialism and the rise of nationalism undermined the old world order, and the sinister forces of fascism and Nazism in Europe and military imperialism in Japan threatened the well-being of humanity around the globe. In the face of it, E. Stanley Jones saw a church splintered by denominational self-interest, unable to offer a united moral witness in the world. His vision of the kingdom of God as the model for humanity called for something better from the body of Christ. In 1940, Jones wrote his powerful book with the probing title, *Is the Kingdom of God Realism?* His bold and clear answer was, of course, affirmative: "Yes! At every turn, it is!"

In order for the church to effectively model God's kingdom, Jones believed that there needed to be a coming together of all churches, for the sake of a united spiritual witness, based on three convictions:

1. Christians are the most united body on earth—if they only know it. "Ironically," Jones said, "the people who are most united at the center are most divided at the circumference."
2. God does not prefer one denomination over another.
3. The expressions of faith that are common to all Christians are varied and diverse.

On this basis, Jones called for a federated union of churches—an organized collective for which each denomination would retain its practices
and traditions, as branches of the Church of Christ in America. Jones
felt that this would give the church a stronger voice on moral issues as it
sought to speak to the world, while still maintaining some of the distinctive emphasis of each branch of the church. He presented his vision in an
article in *Christian Century* magazine, which ended with a rewriting of
the then-familiar Marxist phrase: "Christians of America, unite! We have
nothing to lose except our dividing walls."

Once again, Jones was a man ahead of his times. His proposals—which
he also shared in India, as a vision for the church in that country—were
met with resistance. But in the 1950s and '60s, the ecumenical movement
picked up speed. The World Council of Churches and the National Council of Churches had come into form. The Interchurch Center, often called
the "God Box," at 475 Riverside Drive in New York City, was built in 1958
and was envisioned as the center where mainline Christian churches
would work together. As with Jones' appeal, the voices of the WCC and
the NCC were met with conflict and resistance. Various denominational
mergers failed to produce the hoped-for results, and today, the ecumenical movement as envisioned in the mid-20th century is, essentially, dead.
The "God Box" is almost devoid of denominational leadership.

A 1938 conference held in Madras, India, meant to bring together the
Christian denominations of India, was a disappointment to Jones. Perhaps his criticism of the Tambaram Conference could be leveled at the
church today. His *Christian Century* article was titled, "What I Missed at
Madras." In it, he wrote:

> I missed a church which started from where Jesus started,
> the Kingdom of God, and found instead a church which
> started with itself and therefore, largely ended with itself ...
> dangerously near to fulfilling the statement of Jesus when
> he said, 'he that saveth his life shall lose it.' I missed a
> church which said the Kingdom of God is the hope of the
> church and of the world and found instead a church which
> said, 'I am the hope of the world.' I missed a church loyal to
> the Kingdom of God and found a church loyal to its own
> fellowship.

Thirty years later, E. Stanley Jones wrote an entire book on the nature of the church, entitled, *The Reconstruction of the Church—on What Pattern?* The book sought to share his vision, though we are still left with a divided church in a divided world today. Jones' beloved United Methodist Church is approaching another schism while the world still needs to hear the voice of the churches working together, to "break down the dividing walls of hostility" (Ephesians 2:15).

Though we may never see the kind of organizational federation Jones or the ecumenical movement had in mind, we can seek a spirit of unity which will strengthen our witness in the world in the pattern of the kingdom of God. If we are going to put our arms around the world, we need to begin by putting our arms around each other.

Christians, unite! We have nothing to lose except our dividing walls.

Gracious Father, Thou hast set us within Thy Family, and we would not run away from others. Teach us to enter into loving relationships with one another and to help and be helped in the interplay of life on life. For Thou doest meet us in others. Help us to see Thee in them. Amen.

'Methodism's Pink Fringe'

In the 1950s, during the heat of the Red Scare, *Reader's Digest* published an article entitled "Methodism's Pink Fringe." The article included a criticism of E. Stanley Jones, noting him as a possible Communist sympathizer— or worse. Jones is reported to have responded, with a twinkle in his eye, "Breathes there a man with soul so dead, who never has been called a Red?"

So, the question is worth asking: Was E. Stanley Jones a communist or a socialist?

The question invites a review of his body of work. In 1925 Jones' first book, *The Christ of the Indian Road*, created a stir because of his willingness to learn from the Indian culture and, particularly, Mahatma Gandhi. Jones' call to see Jesus Christ through something other than American and British eyes challenged assumptions of the American church. Between 1933 and 1940, he wrote *Christ and Human Suffering, Christ's Alternative to Communism* and *The Choice Before Us*. Jones specifically addressed American culture in *The Christ of the American Road*, which focused on issues of democracy and the direction of the nation. Unlike many of the preachers of the "holiness movement," out of which he came, Jones was willing to wrestle with issues of culture and politics in a way that was seldom seen—and it led him to conclusions that left many evangelicals uncomfortable.

Howard Snyder, professor of Wesley Studies at Tyndale Seminary in Toronto, Canada and former professor at Asbury Theological Seminary, notes, "He may sound like a socialist when he says, 'The means of production must be in the hands of all for the good of all, rather than in the hands of the few for the exploitation of many,' however, Jones was not arguing for socialism but for Kingdom-of-God economics that combine the dynamism of entrepreneurship with a commitment to civic good."

Snyder also identifies what made Jones distinctive from liberal church voices, on one hand, and conservative evangelicals, on the other:

1. He never lost focus on Jesus Christ, the word made flesh, savior and Lord.
2. He conjoined personal piety and social engagement.
3. He articulated a comprehensive vision of God's kingdom, which combined the present and the future, the personal and social, as well as spiritual and physical dimensions.
4. He saw the essential link between God's kingdom and a visible Christian community.
5. He remained grounded in Scripture.

A trip to Russia in 1935 had a major effect on Jones. Reflecting on the trip, he wrote:

> What I saw in Russia so deeply impressed me that I felt as never before that this was the problem we would have to face in the future. I know there are two sides to the question of Russia: There is poverty, the lack of liberty, the drive against religion. But there is another side: the enthusiasm of the people who believe that they have the truth that will hold the future and the self-sacrifice of all classes to make a new Russia in which all have a share in the good life. We must choose, on a world-wide scale, whether we shall make the future after the pattern of Marx or after the pattern of Jesus and the Kingdom of God.

Clearly, much has changed in Russia and the former Soviet Union since 1935. One can only wonder what Jones would make of it now. At the time, however, the experience in Russia led Jones to a deep reflection on the meaning of the kingdom of God and the writing of *Christ's Alternative to Communism*, a year later.

For Jones, it ultimately boiled down to this: Everything—including politics, economics, the church and the whole of life—needs to be measured by the values of the kingdom of God, with the life of Jesus Christ as the pattern. Economically, Jesus' emphasis on the needs of the poor should become one of the highest priorities. Even today some may call this "socialism," but for Jones, it was simply the living out of the Gospel. As Snyder says, "Jones was prophetic in insisting that God's reign is not just an ideal or solely a future or otherworldly reality. It is a present reality and agenda for both church and society."

So, to answer the question: Was E. Stanley Jones a communist or a socialist?

Jones himself declared:

> I am not a Communist, nor do I call myself a Socialist, but I am a Christian seeking for a solution of this problem. I am sure—desperately sure—that Christianity must give a lead at this time or abdicate. It is not enough to tell me that Christianity can and does change the lives of individual men. Shall we rescue individual slaves and leave intact the slave system? Shall we reclaim individual drunkards and not touch the liquor traffic? Shall we pick up the wounded in war and leave intact the war system?

Jones was convinced the Gospel was not just applicable to the individual, but to the whole of society—and that Christians were called to both personal experience and social witness.

If Jones were alive today, I am sure he would have joined Martin Luther King, Jr. and John Lewis in the vision of the "Beloved Community," believing that would be the fulfillment of the kingdom of God. Living the values of the kingdom of God should take precedence over all other loyalties, even if it appears to be "the pink fringe."

In the end, it's all about the kingdom.

O God, Thou hast a plan for our nation. Help us as a people humbly to surrender to Thy plan and work it out. For if we take our way, we shall lose our way. If we take Thy way, we shall find ours. Amen.

Judson Collins, the first
Methodist missionary
to China, in 1847.

E. Stanley Jones with a plaque in Central
Methodist Church, Lucknow, India.

A Crisis of Health
and Faith

The challenges faced by international missionaries in the 19th and early 20th century were monumental. Not only was travel difficult, but communication was limited and the demands of living in a strange culture could be overwhelming. Contact with family and friends in the United States happened primarily by mail, which sometimes took weeks to be delivered. Strange food, harsh climate and language barriers, let alone diseases like malaria, were constant burdens.

In 1847, a young Judson Collins left Michigan as the first Methodist missionary to China. He was there only four years, came home desperately ill, and died at age 29.

"Many missionaries' health broke before their first ten-year term was completed," notes biographer Robert Tuttle, adding, "Stanley was one of them."

For Stanley Jones, the workload—coupled with his driven personality—contributed to a series of nervous collapses after more than eight years in India. The pressures were taking their toll. His body was no longer throwing off infections like tetanus and his stress-induced weakness had increased. Even while preaching, his mind would sometimes go blank and he would be forced to sit down, embarrassed and perplexed. Eventually, he was ordered by the mission board to return to America for an early furlough. As Tuttle states, "He had not finished his first ten-year term, but he was finished."

The Jones family started back to the U.S. in March of 1916. Because of the war, they journeyed east, from India, through Singapore and Hong Kong. There, they caught a steamer for California by way of Japan and Hawaii. The trip took three months.

Even during the furlough year, Stanley traveled the country with speaking engagements and raised funds; Mabel and their 2-year-old daughter, Eunice, rested. In 1917, the family headed back to India. Following the three-month trip back to India, Stanley's strength still was not renewed. He took two retreats at Sat Tal, but felt he simply could not continue.

At this low point Jones attended a worship service at the Central Methodist Church in Lucknow, where Rev. Tamil David was preaching. In a time of prayer, he said, "Lord, I'm done for. I've reached the end of my resources and I can't go on." Once again, as at other times in his life, Jones sensed a calming inner voice. This inner voice relayed, "If you will turn your problems over to me, I will take care of you." In simple faith, he said, "Lord, I chose the bargain right here"—and in that moment, he knew he was on the path to healing and wholeness once again. Today, a marble plaque in the church in Lucknow reads: "Here Dr. E. Stanley Jones, world evangelist, surrendered his physically shattered life to Christ and rose a whole man."

Robert Tuttle summarizes the meaning of the event:

> In Stanley's own words, he had moved from 'weakness to strength, from confusion to certainty, from inner conflict to unity, from myself to His Self.' Before, he doubted he would have the ability to carry on. Now he would rely on the Spirit's resources. He had started with so little, now he needed so much. But now, he would no longer rely on his own resources, he would be exclusively reliant upon the Holy Spirit.

Jones would look back at this moment as a turning point in his life and ministry. Even though he continued his almost nonstop traveling at an unimaginable pace, he found more balance and better control in his life.

In his renewed relationship with God, Jones found the resources he lacked and carried on his work for succeeding decades.

In the second Corinthian letter, St. Paul describes something of the same experience. He says that he complained to God three times about the "thorn in his flesh." We don't know exactly what the thorn was; some people believe he was epileptic, while others suggest that the thorn was his lack of self-confidence, because he was short in stature. Most preachers think it was probably some cantankerous church member's constant criticism. Whatever it was, St. Paul says that he heard God say, "My grace is sufficient for you. My strength is made perfect in your weakness" (II Corinthians 12:9). As far as we know, the thorn never left him—but instead, he found strength in spite of his weakness.

There are moments when, like Jones, we feel like saying, "I'm done for. I can't go on." In these moments, his witness inspires us to discover grace beyond our comprehension—the ability to go on and thrive, with God's strength working in and through our weakness.

O blessed, blessed Jesus, Thou hast turned all my sunsets into sunrises, all my gloom into glory, all my doubts into delights. Thou art the Great Illumination. Amen.

Falling Into the Arms of Grace

"Along the way, I have learned the art of falling well."
—E. Stanley Jones

E. Stanley Jones suffered a massive stroke in his 87th year, which left him partially paralyzed and with limited speech. Even so, he managed to write his final book with the anticipated title, *The Divine Yes*. It was based on St. Paul's resounding affirmation: "The divine 'yes' has, at last, sounded in Christ. For in him is the 'yes' that affirms all the promises of God" (II Corinthians 1:19-20, Moffatt translation).

"I believe God is saying to me, 'I am handing you back your life for a demonstration period at the very end, so that a viewer looking in may see if there is anything in it,'" said Jones. To Eunice, he said, "Daughter, I cannot die now. I have to complete another book—*The Divine Yes!*"

Looking back, Jones described a moment (at Sat Tal Ashram) when he had "fallen well": he tripped on a stone protruding into the pathway and took "a dive straight forward, like a dive into second base in baseball, on the gravel path," said Jones. "I picked myself up and searched for hurts and bruises but didn't find any. I said, 'All is well,' and went on to the group." Jones' conclusion was this: "Along the way, I have learned the art of falling well. Usually, I have managed to fall forward."

For him, it became a parable of the final days of his life. According to Jones:

When I came to the fall—the autumn—of my life and this stroke which left me in shambles, I knew that the only Christian way to fall was to fall on my knees and thank God that though outwardly I am only a half a person, in Him I am whole and well and the same person I was before. If I had to choose between the two alternatives of being a half person inwardly and whole outwardly, or a half person outwardly and a whole person inwardly, I would choose the latter. I have fallen, but I have fallen into the arms of Grace.

Along the path, there will be times when life trips us up; times when we are surprised by the sudden bumps and bruises that come our way. At some point, all of us will face the final fall of death—either in old age, with declining abilities, or as an abbreviated life cut short too soon. Either way, to fall knowing we are falling into the arms of grace gives courage and hope.

In one of my churches, we had a member of the custodial staff who, in spite of some limitations, served well and was a philosopher of sorts. Every day, when I entered the building, he would say, "Good morning, Dr. Harnish. Everyone has some bumps in the road, don't they, Dr. Harnish?" I would answer, "Yes, Mike, everyone has bumps in the road." Then he would always ask the probing question: "Why is that, Dr. Harnish? Why does everyone have bumps in the road?" In all honesty, I had to respond, "I don't know, Mike. We just do."

Philosopher Mike was right, of course. We all have bumps in the road, and usually there are no answers to the "Why?" question. Instead, the essential question is "How?" When we trip on the bumps in the road, *how* do we fall? From Stanley Jones, we can learn the art of falling well—the ability to fall forward, with the assurance that we are falling into the arms of grace.

O God, I know I cannot run away from Thee, for I cannot run away from myself. For I am fashioned for Thee, and Thou art the life of my life, the joy of my joy, the being of my being. Nor do I want to run away; I want to run into Thy arms. For there I am home. Amen.

Always Ascending

In his autobiography, Stanley Jones begins the introduction with his characteristic sense of humor:

> I laugh at myself as I take my pen—my pen, not a typewriter, though that would be easier—to begin to rewrite *A Song of Ascents*, my spiritual autobiography. I say to myself, 'How absurd can you be? You're eighty-three and you are beginning a third attempt to write that autobiography.'

He had already tried twice, and the second manuscript was 560 pages long. But Jones rejected both attempts. The third time, instead of simply writing an autobiography describing the events of his life, he determined he would write what he called a "spiritual autobiography." This would set him "in the midst of life, sharing the same basic needs and problems as others," as opposed to setting himself apart as a unique person. As is characteristic of Jones' work, his humility and desire to connect with men and women at a human and authentic level is reflected in the pages of that book.

The title comes from Psalms 120-134, referred to as "Song of Ascents" because the psalms were sung by Jewish pilgrims on their way to worship at the ancient temple in Jerusalem. Since the temple sat on the highest point of land, worshippers literally *ascended* to the temple. If you begin in

the wilderness at the Dead Sea, the lowest point on earth, and you make
your way toward the holy city and the Temple Mount, it is one steady
climb—ever upward—until you arrive at the place of worship. Jones chose
that image to describe his life's journey:

> I shall sing my song of the pilgrimage I am making, from
> what I was to what God is making of me. I say, 'What God is
> making of me,' for the best I can say about myself is that I am
> a Christian in-the-making. Not yet 'made,' but only in-the-
> making, at eighty-three. I am glad I am not 'made,' for there
> is joy and anticipation in 'being made.'

Jones continues, "I begin this third attempt with a solid joy and antic-
ipation, for I have a feeling I have struck the right note, the note of a
willingness to say 'I'm sorry, I'm wrong. I am beginning over again.' People
who are always right are always wrong—wrong in their very attitude about
always being right."

Part of the beauty of E. Stanley Jones' life was his willingness to grow,
to change, to learn and to continue the journey, as long as he lived. After
writing 27 wildly popular books, lecturing on every continent, being
acclaimed by religious and political leaders alike and serving as a counselor to U.S. presidents and other world leaders, he still considered himself
to be "on the way," still "in-the-making," still ascending. Though he was
clear about his own unwavering convictions concerning Jesus Christ, he
remained open to what he might learn from people he met along the way.

Therefore, Jones describes his life as a type of song of ascents. He cap-
italized the word "song" to make his point: "It is a Song, not a song or a
ditty to divert you from reality, but a Song which has behind it the music
of the spheres; the sum total of reality is behind the Song. I sing because I
have something to sing about, but my something is a Someone. My theme
Song is Jesus Christ."

No matter how old we are or how long we have been on the journey,
we are still in-the-making, still being made, always under construction,
always ascending.

And the song we sing is a song of ascent.

O God, I am so grateful that Thou hast promised to enlarge my margins. I have been living on skimpy resources, have been scraping the bottom of my barrel. Now give me life abundantly. Amen.

Contagious, Cosmic Laughter

Whenever someone asked the great African American preacher Peter Gomes how he was, instead of the standard "I'm fine," he would reply, "I flourish!" E. Stanley Jones would agree. In his quiet, gentle way, the man radiated unquenchable joy. He flourished!

In one of his sermons, he shared this delightful story:

> I was up in Alaska, writing a book between meetings and I had to write sitting in front of a mirror because there was no other place to write. I stopped my writing and looked into the looking glass and saw myself. I said, 'Stanley Jones, you are a very happy man, aren't you?' I said, 'Yes, I am very happy.' And I asked, 'How did you get that way?' I said, 'I don't know. I walked across a field one day and I stubbed my toe and said, "What's this treasure?"' I ran off and sold everything I had and bought the field. I've been hugging myself ever since.

Jones was actually retelling a parable of Jesus, recorded in Matthew 13:44—a parable told in just one sentence: "The kingdom of heaven is like treasure hidden in a field, which someone found and hid; then, in his joy, he goes and sells all he has and buys that field."

That's it. That's all Jesus said. He leaves us asking questions like, "What treasure?" "Which field?" "If he already had the treasure, why did he buy the field?" Jones was obviously referring to his own conversion and his journey in the Christian life, but just like Jesus, he tells it in such simplicity that it leaves us to ponder what it meant for him and what it can mean for us. In short, he found joy. That is all that matters.

The irony is this paragraph comes from a sermon about self-surrender, another one of Jones' favorite topics. From the title, you might think that the sermon would be heavy on the demanding discipline of surrendering your will to some other power—in this case, the lordship of Jesus Christ. For Jones, however, there is nothing but joy to be found in the act of surrender. He says:

> It is a paradox. I can't explain it. But when you lose your life, you find it. You are never as much your own as when you are most His. Belonging to Jesus, you belong to yourself.

In Jones' last book, he tells of a conversation with a therapist who was trying to help him walk, following his stroke. The therapist said, "You have the most contagious laughter I have ever heard." He responded, "Contagious laughter?" Comments Jones:

> It was the first time it was ever said of me, but it could be said of me now. I laugh and the world laughs with me. I have cosmic backing for my laughter. I am saying this with laughter at the closing of my life.

One of the last entries in *The Divine Yes* includes a wonderful example of Jones' delightful sense of humor, from a sermon he preached in 1973 at Sat Tal Ashram: "I have often said that when the people stand around and say, 'Well, Brother Stanley is gone,' I want to be able to wink at them, and if I have enough strength, I would like to laugh and say, 'Jesus is Lord.' Because it will not be death, it will be fuller life."

Contagious, cosmic laughter.

O Christ, my every thought dances and sings when it thinks of Thee. For Thou hast set Joy within my heart. I knew some joy before I found Thee. But in Thee I know Joy, and in that Joy all lesser joys are contained and come to fulfillment. Am I grateful? Read my unspoken gratitude. Amen.

And the World Still Waits

"It should come as no surprise that Stanley Jones played a key role in some of the most significant historical and political issues of his time, events that continue to shape the world today."

—Biographer Robert Tuttle

Particularly in his early years, much of Jones' ministry was focused on India. As the move toward independence from British rule progressed, Bishop J. Wascom Pickett said, of Jones and his influence: "Probably no non-Indian contributed more to the development of the strong moral and ethical sentiment that characterized Indian national leadership and the formation of the Constitution of India." Yet Jones' efforts for peace extended around the world, with emphasis also in the United States.

In 1941 Jones was on an exhausting American evangelistic tour, speaking between two and five times each day. Even in the midst of his demanding schedule, he was keenly aware of the growing tension between the U.S. and Japan. Jones was convinced there were opportunities for the United States to work for peace; he knew that there were people in Japan who felt the same. For Jones, the vision of the kingdom of God called for a world free of violence and war, following the pattern of Ephesians 2:14-16: "For he is our peace who has made the two groups one and has broken down the dividing walls of hostility to create in himself one new humanity out of two, thus making peace."

Interrupting his tour of the West Coast, Jones traveled to Washington, D.C. to meet with congressmen, businessmen and a variety of peace groups, proposing that the U.S. function as the mediator of a new world order. He worked with Toyohiko Kagawa, a famous Japanese Christian leader, to create dialogue that might resolve the escalating tension between the two nations. Jones' proposal was published in the Congressional Record, read by the secretary of state and included in materials sent to the president. It was also sent to 100,000 pastors and church leaders, which resulted in the creation of the Churchmen's Campaign for Peace through Mediation.

In his autobiography, Jones writes, "So I went to Washington, going out like Abraham not knowing whither I was going." Between September and December, Jones spent three days a week in Washington as an unofficial negotiator among diplomats from Japan, China and the U.S., shuttling between the White House and the special Japanese envoys who were trying to ease the conflict. He met with President Franklin D. Roosevelt on Dec. 3, 1941, encouraging him to send a message to the Japanese emperor with a proposal for peace. The cable was finally sent on Dec. 5, but it did not reach the emperor until after the Dec. 7 attack on Pearl Harbor. According to Robert Tuttle, it was later reported that the emperor said if he had received the cable earlier, he would have called off the attack. Stephen Graham raises the question: "Did Stanley Jones almost single-handedly come within a hair's breadth of preventing the Japanese attack on Pearl Harbor?" It seems the answer might be "Yes."

Jones' failure to help negotiate a way to avoid the war with Japan was one of his greatest disappointments. Years later, when he wrote his autobiographical *A Song of Ascents*, he devoted an entire chapter to it. The chapter is called "Guidance—An Adventure in Failure." In it, he concludes:

> Our best endeavors are often not good enough. I wrote it off as an adventure in failure. It is not ours to succeed or fail. It is ours to do the highest we know and leave the results to God.

In 1950, Stanley once again tried his hand at shuttle diplomacy—this time, out of fear that the Korean War might escalate. He carried a proposal from India to Washington, visited with members of Congress and the state department, and spent 15 minutes with President Harry Truman. Once again nothing came of his efforts, but these examples represent the reach of Jones' influence and his unflagging efforts for reconciliation and peace.

Back in India, Stanley's commitment to seeking pathways to brotherhood took on a particular focus as he and his missionary wife, Mabel, worked diligently to encourage reconciliation between Muslims and Hindus. It was Stanley's hope the new, independent India could model a society in which diverse religions lived side-by-side. Again, his vision still awaits fulfillment. Today, the tension between Hindus and Muslims continues to escalate.

Since the time of E. Stanley Jones, America has found itself caught up in a seemingly endless series of wars and conflicts. The challenge for Christian leaders is to put their arms around the world, as agents of reconciliation—a need that is as urgent today as it was in the 1940s.

And the world still waits.

O God, in a world torn and fragmented, help me to heal everything I touch, and help me to touch everything. Give me the healing hands and the healing heart. For Thou art sending me to reconcile everywhere. Amen.

DR. STANLEY JONES

KRISTUS
MAAILMA TEEDEL

EESTISTANUD
MAG. SALME KLAOS

KIRJASTUS „KRISTLIK KAITSJA"
TARTU, 1936

E. Stanley Jones' *The Christ of Every Road*,
published in Estonia in 1936, prior to the Soviet
occupation and the banning of religious books.

Banned Books and Rebirth

Meeli Tankler was a youth growing up in Estonia during the years of Communist oppression, when it was part of the Soviet Union. The publication of religious books was banned and most had been destroyed.

There was hope, however.

"Some people managed to hide books and shared them with fellow Christians," said Tankler. "I still remember the pure joy of reading *The Christ of Every Road* in Estonian as a teenager. Thus, Jones became one of my first spiritual mentors in the midst of an openly atheist society."

Jones' books, *Christ and Human Suffering* and *The Christ of Every Road*, had been translated into Estonian in 1935 and 1936. During those years of Estonian independence, both books were widely circulated and read by Christians of various denominations. When the Soviets came in 1941, they ordered all books considered "ideologically wrong"—including religious books—destroyed. Some brave Christians managed to hide their copies, though, and secretly shared them with trustworthy Christians. Copies were made on typewriters, which were very rare at the time, or handwritten.

The same was true of hymnals. This handwritten songbook was secretly used by Estonian Methodists to teach the faith to their children. Since most of the Soviet Russian leadership did not speak Estonian, they assumed that the Estonians were teaching the children to sing traditional folk songs, which were a large part of the Estonian culture. Thus, the faith was passed on in secret.

During the Soviet years, 17 small Methodist congregations managed to survive in Estonia. It was the only place in the Soviet Union where the Methodist Church—which had been present throughout the region—was able to carry on under the Communist regime. Pastors and leaders were frequently harassed and intimidated. Some were sent to prison and even martyred for their faith. Rev. Aleksander Kumm was the pastor of the Methodist Church in Tallinn during the second world war, and he was there when the church building was destroyed by Soviet bombing in 1944. In 1952, he was sent to live in Siberia for four years. Courageously, he returned to lead the church as a pastor and superintendent until his death.

In 1960, while still under Soviet control, someone managed to translate *The Christ of the Mount* into Estonian. Since it could not be published, copies were once again typed or copied by hand. Tankler says, "I have held in my own hands the hand-written copy of this book, which is in three thick notebooks." Her husband, Rev. Ullas Tankler, used it as a resource for Bible study classes in his Methodist congregation in the 1980s. It was finally published in Estonian in 1990, after the fall of the Soviet Union and the coming of Estonian independence. "With so few books by Christian authors available in the Estonian language," said Meeli, "*The Christ of the Mount* became a valuable resource for many Christians and still is. So the legacy of E. Stanley Jones is alive in Estonia today."

Jones' legacy lives on not only in his books, but in the lives of Estonian Methodists. In 1994 the United Methodist Church established the Baltic Methodist Theological Seminary in Tallinn, to train leadership for the Christian churches of the Baltic states. Meeli Tankler recently retired as the rector of the seminary, and she continues to serve there. Her husband, Rev. Ullas Tankler, is an ordained elder in the Estonian Methodist Church and is currently the regional director for Europe, Eurasia and North Africa, as in on the General Board of Global Ministries of the United Methodist Church.

Throughout Eastern Europe, Russia and the Baltic states, the church is coming back to life after the dark years of Communist domination—and E. Stanley Jones' banned books are contributing to the rebirth.

O God, Thou whose Almighty hand hath led us thus far on the way, guide us to the consummation of our destiny—a world federal union. For Thou art guiding us, we feel it in our bones. In Jesus' name, amen.

Note: Jones' vision of a "federal union" of churches never materialized, but this prayer reflects his hope for a world united, a world at peace. For more information on the Baltic Methodist Theological Seminary, go to emkts.ee.

Hand-copied children's songbook. Photo courtesy of Rev. Lavere Webster, Wesley Collection, First United Methodist Church, Birmingham, Mich.

E. Stanley Jones' body being
carried into his funeral, in India

And What About Death?

As Jones faced old age and the reality of death, he faced it with the same confidence which had marked his life. In *A Song of Ascents*, he writes:

> So I stand assured, assured that neither encroaching time
> nor approaching death can touch me—the real me—for I do
> not belong to time or to death. I belong to the timeless and
> to the deathless: I belong to Jesus Christ. I know that I shall
> have to surrender my body to what they call death, for I
> know I live in a mortal world. Death is a part of life. I accept
> it and I trust I will welcome it when it comes. But while a
> part of me will submit to time and death, the real me will be
> intact because I belong to the immortal Jesus Christ.

Jones then hypothesizes about what will happen after death, in a paragraph that demonstrates his wit as well as his confidence in the Christian way of life:

> Am I daydreaming? Suppose I come to the end of this life
> and find there is nothing beyond death except a vast cipher
> 0—nothing. If that comes to pass, I will look at the universe
> and say, 'You have disappointed me, for I thought you had
> meaning and purpose. But now I see there is nothing but a

vast Nothing. Well, of course, I thought better of you, but I do not repent of being a Christian.' Future or no future, the Christian way is the best way to live. Like the old woman who said, 'If I got up to heaven and they wouldn't let me in, I would shout all around the walls, "Well, I've had a wonderful time coming!"'

As part of his faith in Jesus Christ and the Resurrection, Jones did, in fact, believe there would be life beyond death. "If not," he writes, "where will I grow up? I've just begun to learn how to live." Yet Jones admitted more than once that we have no clear understanding about what happens after death. Still, he was convinced that faith in Christ would carry him into new life, as promised in the resurrection of Jesus Christ. In the meantime, his focus was on what it means to live in the *now*, to experience heaven in this life by living in the presence of the living Christ and seeking to discover the kingdom of God at work in the world. He believed the gift of resurrection after death would be the fulfillment of what one experiences in this life, trusting that the same faith he held during his life would hold him beyond the grave.

One of Jones' colorful images of the afterlife conveys his focus on ministry, in fulfillment of the calling he had received so many years before. He imagines his arrival in heaven:

> If I keep my present state of mind and purpose, I will ask for twenty-four hours of rest after I arrive in heaven. Then I will ask for twenty-four hours to visit with my friends. Then I would like to go up to Jesus and say, 'This is wonderful, and I don't deserve to be here; grace has brought me home and I love it here. But haven't you a world that is fallen, that needs an evangelist? Please send me.' For I know no heaven more heavenly than proclaiming the good news of Jesus Christ.'

After his stroke, with the help of his family and friends, Jones was able to make one last trip to his beloved India. It was there he died, on January 25, 1973. Part of his ashes and his heart of love were buried in the soil of India and the rest of his ashes were returned to Baltimore, to be buried in the bishops' lot at Mount Olivet Cemetery. So his journey had come full circle: from the day he knelt at the altar of Memorial Methodist Episcopal

Church in Baltimore, to the day he was returned there for his final rest. In between, he had spent his life putting his arms around the world. Like Brother Stanley, until the day we make our final journey, we are called to do the same.

For E. Stanley Jones, death, as Paul says, was "swallowed up in victory. O grave, where is thy victory? O death, where is thy sting? Thanks be to God who gives us the victory through our Lord Jesus Christ" (I Corinthians 15).

O Deathless Christ, alive forevermore, why should I be afraid of death? I am in Thee, and death becomes unbelievably unimportant, a mere transition, a veranda that opens to the House of Many Rooms. Amen.

Stanley and Mabel Jones in their later years, in Iowa.

Saluting the Dawn
with a Cheer

"We went to the hospital expecting to visit a sick old man. Instead, we found Dr. Jones exciting and challenging."

—Rev. Charles Yoost, retired pastor emeritus at Church of the Saviour in Cleveland, Ohio

Rev. Charles Yoost was a student at Boston University School of Theology when E. Stanley Jones had the massive stroke that would ultimately end his life. At that time Jones was in rehabilitation and getting restless, so a group of seminary students was invited to visit him. When they got there, they found not a sick old man, but a spirited evangelist who had prepared for their visit and ended up actually teaching the seminary class from his hospital bed. He lectured them every Monday for about six weeks.

Typical of the influence Jones had on students around the world, the lives and ministries of this small group of seminary students were forever impacted by the time they spent with Jones. Yoost recalls:

> Although he was recovering from the stroke, Stanley Jones was fully alive at 88. He was partially paralyzed, but his faith and zeal were as strong as ever. He told us about his stroke and how he interpreted it in the light of his faith. Then, he told us, of all things, about his plans for the future!

At the time, Jones was planning to write one more book, *The Divine Yes*. Yoost says Jones told the students, "How can I write on the Divine Yes when my body is saying 'No'? Then he laughed! And so he continued to write the book, which would be his last word to the world."

As Yoost noted, Jones spoke with enviable passion:

He became so intense in his speech and so excited that his voice became high-pitched and incomprehensible. Imagine that. A person so excited about the Christian faith that, at 88 he can hardly control his voice. I went away from his room that day feeling that the life of a man who was still excited about his message after preaching it for 70 years was certainly a living witness to the Christian faith.

The same passion and zeal these students experienced near the end of Jones' life could be felt throughout his life, from beginning to end. One of Jones' most popular devotional books was called *Abundant Living*, and for him it was not just the title of a book but the theme of his personal life and work. In the preface to the book, he writes, "Everyone may and can live abundantly. The business of life is to live and to live well and adequately and abundantly. Instead, we have picked the flowers of life to pieces, petal by petal, and have lost its beauty in the process."

As Jones approached the last stage of life, he continued to live abundantly despite his limitations. His final witness would be words of passion for the Gospel and the promise of life beyond the grave—a dawn yet to come. A prayer from *Abundant Living* reflects that enduring hope:

O Christ, we thank Thee that the last word is not useless regrets over the defeated yesterdays, or the difficult days, but the last word is the dawning tomorrows. With Thee, 'the best is yet to be.' We salute the Dawn with a cheer! For we have the Dawn within us. Amen.

For E. Stanley Jones, the last word was a word of hope.
The word was "dawn"—and he greeted it with a cheer.

O Christ, I thank Thee that in betting my life on Thee I can't lose. For if there is no future, I win now. I win, for I've found in Thee Life. What can lesser life do to Life? I am immortal even if there is no immortality. I thank Thee. Amen.

Note: Charles Yoost is currently the director of religious life and church outreach at Lakeside Chautauqua, in Ohio. Jones visited Lakeside four times in five decades; his first visit was in 1924, and his last was in 1968. Information on his visits can be found in the archives at Lakeside.

E. Stanley Jones at an ashram in Wisconsin.

30

I Can Still Hear His Voice

Cliff Bath was 32 and unemployed the first time he met E. Stanley Jones. Looking back, the 90-year-old retired businessman and dedicated Christian recalls:

> When I met E. Stanley Jones, I was mesmerized by his words. He had a way of just rolling out his words and his stories which was captivating. Even today, when I read his books he comes to life and I feel his presence. His English accent (probably coming from his time in India) and the roll of his words were like no one else I have ever heard.

The first time Bath heard him speak, Jones used one of the comments he frequently repeated in his lectures. Bath remembers him saying, "Show me something better and I will buy it. But until then, it is Christ for me." It has stuck with Bath all these years.

In 1963 Jones and Bath rode together in a car for several hours, as Bath drove Jones from Ohio to Detroit for a speaking engagement. This was at the rise of the Civil Rights movement, and during the ride they talked about Martin Luther King, Jr. and the credit he gave Jones for commitment to nonviolence (which he had gleaned from reading Jones' book on Gandhi). In his genuine humility, Jones said, "Now that's quite something, isn't it?"

Jones, however, was much more concerned about Bath's unemployment and the issues which brought it about. Bath told Jones that he had left the company because he could no longer accept the questionable ethics of the owner, a prominent businessman who was nationally known in motor racing.

Two years later, Bath attended a breakfast at which Jones was speaking. He was amazed when Jones recognized him immediately and said, "Cliff Bath, I've wondered how you were doing. I never forget a man with a story." The story, of course, was of his courage in leaving a position of responsibility on the basis of ethical convictions. In the years that followed, Bath heard Jones speak several times. He was also present when Jones conducted a healing service in his home church in Detroit. It was a friendship that would have a lasting impact on a multitude of people far beyond those first encounters.

Bath recalled one more interesting anecdote from Jones' visit to Detroit, this one involving the great evangelist's humility. According to Bath, Jones was booked to stay at the upscale Book Cadillac Hotel in Detroit, with the expenses being paid by a donor. As he checked in, he made the comment, "You know, I am just a poor missionary"—and at his request, he was assigned to a small, dismal back room in the hotel. He said the same thing over dinner, as the reason for not ordering dessert, until he found out it was included in the price of the meal. "Then," Bath relays, "he enjoyed it immensely!"

Jones' influence has had a lasting impact on the world through the lives of people like Cliff Bath, and many of those stories will never be told. Beyond his business, Bath has dedicated his life to various ministries that are making a significant difference in the city of Detroit. One of those ministries is Cass Community United Methodist Church and Cass Community Social Services. Since the days of the Great Depression the Cass community has worked in the inner city, feeding the hungry and providing care for the homeless. Under the leadership of Rev. Faith Fowler, Cass has evolved into a major ministry in the city, housing 350 people per night and providing over 1 million meals a year; offering jobs in their "green industries" for formerly unemployed people; and building tiny homes for the formerly homeless.

Bath has been a guide and donor for Cass and other ministries throughout the years, simply living out what E. Stanley Jones taught him many years ago. Recently, he has been involved with the E. Stanley Jones Foundation in the republication of Jones' books, so that his work can live on through a generation of dedicated men and women like Cliff Bath—all influenced by Jones' ministry.

Looking back through the years, Bath notes, "He was a person you just never forget. Remember the song, 'He touched me and now I am no longer the same'? Well, once I met E. Stanley Jones, I was never the same—and after all these years, when I read his writings, I can still hear his voice."

O Christ, Thou who art the Way. From my depths I thank Thee that I am on an Endless Way, with endless Resources, with endless Happiness, with endless Gratitude, under the process of an endless Growth. I thank Thee, thank Thee. Amen.

Note: Thanks to the work of the E. Stanley Jones Foundation, his voice can still be heard. CDs of a collection of Jones' sermons are available at EStanleyJonesFoundation.com, along with many of his books, which have recently been republished. For information on Cass Community Social Services, visit CassCommunity.org.

Jones with a group of children.

Still Pretty Good

Mary John Dye and Sandy Sheppherd were students at Asbury College in the 1970s. Together, they shared childhood memories of E. Stanley Jones: Mary John's father was a pastor in Kentucky, and Sandy's father was a missionary in India. Jones would often visit their homes in Frankfort, Kentucky and in Belgaum, India. As Sheppherd recalls, "When he would visit our home, I would follow him around as he prayed. Late every afternoon the white-haired man would repeat the ritual. With hands clasped behind his back, head bowed in thought, Uncle Stanley walked around the path and slowly strolled among the huge banyan trees, silently pondering his next sermon or praying as he walked."

As a little girl, Sheppherd would follow Stanley: with her hands clasped behind her back in imitation, she carefully measured every step. Finally, he would turn around and, with a warm smile, take her hand—and together, they would stroll back to the mission house.

Rev. Mary John Dye, now senior pastor of Triplett UMC, Mooresville, NC, has a different memory.

"When I was growing up, E. Stanley Jones was a frequent preacher in my father's churches.," she said. "In fact, he spent his 80th birthday in our home. When he came down to breakfast that morning, he said he was just rereading one of his devotional books we had placed in the guestroom.

With his genuinely humble spirit and a sheepish, playful grin, he added, 'And it is still pretty good.'"

Jones was referring to one of his numerous books of daily readings, which sold millions of copies in multiple languages and inspired the daily lives of men and women around the world. His first devotional book, *The Way*, was originally published in 1946 and has been reprinted several times—and is still pretty good. Here is a quotation from the reading, entitled, "Life Reduced to Simplicity":

> You can be rich in two ways: in the abundance of your possessions or in the fewness of your wants. When your wants are reduced to simplicity, you are rich. Our definition of Christianity then becomes simple. Complicated creeds and systems give way to the simple. A very pompous bishop asked some village people in India who were candidates for baptism, "What is it to be a Christian?" He expected a theological reply, but instead, they said, "To live like Mr. Murphy." Mr. Murphy was the missionary who had taught them. The Word had become flesh in Mr. Murphy. O living Christ, make me simple, unaffected and unafraid. Give me the mind that was in Thee, then I, too, shall be simple, straightforward and loving. I would have a heart that loves the simple and the true. Give me that heart.

Rev. Mary John Dye also recalls, "Even though I was so young at the time, I remember he was a truly godly man with a Christ-centered focus for everything he did. It is a great gift for a child or a family or a congregation or a denomination to know such saints personally. I was truly blessed."

Another witness to Jones' impact on young lives is Sarah Parker. She attended one of Jones' ashrams as a youth, at Eastern Nazarene College. The next ashram included a message by Tom Carruth, who frequently traveled with Jones. Parker says, "That was when I felt called to the mission field"—and she has spent her life in missionary service, literally putting her arms around the world in the spirit of E. Stanley Jones.

Jones' impact on the world, through both his speaking and his writing, is unquestionable. But perhaps the most important measure of his ministry would be his influence on individuals like Mary John Dye, Sandy

Sheppherd and Sarah Parker. His humble spirit gave him the ability to connect with people of every age, in every culture and on every walk of life, from presidents and emperors to common folks and children; from the "untouchables" of the lowest caste to the highly educated intellectuals of India.

From our vantage point, five decades after his death, some of Jones' writing may seem a bit dated. Yet his ability to make his message accessible to all can be seen in everything he wrote—and much of it still applicable today. His words for readers in the 1940s could have been written for Christian disciples of the 21st century:

> You are in the hour of pruning, the pruning of the extraneous, the unnecessary and the wrong. Ask God to give you clear insight and courageous decisiveness. You have come to the crossroads, one road leading to complication upon complication, the other leading to simplicity and sureness. Surrender all that complicates your life into the hands of God.

And, 70 years later, it is still pretty good.

O Christ, I see. I have been nervous and anxious and complicated. And now at long last I am coming to the simple. I am in union with Thee. That is my primary and only responsibility. I accept it with joy. I am a child again, simple, happy, unafraid. Amen.

Afterword

The Rev. Dr. E. Stanley Jones accepted a call to mission in 1903 when he accepted a calling to India at the age of 23 years old. Jones should rightfully be considered a pioneer for the people called Methodist in India. In addition, he occupies a significant role in the Protestant Church's relations with the Non-Western world and the Indian faith agent for social change, Mahatma Gandhi.

It is clear that the Western world owes Jones an enormous debt of gratitude for engaging the Indian culture, world, and faith experience for which none was prepared. To this end, Dr. Anne Mathews-Younes, President of the E. Stanley Jones Foundation, tells of her grandfather's evangelical zeal and engagement with Non-Western religion in India. On a 20-hour train ride from Bombay to Lucknow, Jones enthusiastically read an account of Jesus' Sermon on the Mount to an English-speaking Muslim gentleman. Jones, expecting the man to be overwhelmed, was struck to the core when he heard the response: "We have the same thing in our Sacred Book!" Mathers-Younes says, "This 'all religions are the same—only the paths are different' attitude so widely held by many in the non-Christian world, shook Jones, as he wasn't prepared to deal with such attitudes."

Dr. Mathews-Younes' says her grandfather chose to present India with "a disentangled Christ, apart from the trappings of Christianity, apart from Western Civilization ... a universal Christ, belonging to all cultures and races and the answer to all human need." For Jones, it was not the superiority of Christ above other faiths and religions, but rather the all-sufficiency of Christ that formed the foundation. Significantly, then, it was the embrace of the Christ that enabled Jones to relate to the life, work, and witness of Gandhi.

Jones' invitation for "putting one's arms around the world" comes from a close encounter with knowing the open arms of the Universe that took in both his faith and Mahatma Gandhi's philosophy of life—Satyagraha.

Gandhi used the term "Satyagraha" according to its roots from the Sanskrit and Hindi concepts of "*satya*," denoting "love and firmness in a good cause" while "*agraha*" means "a force that holds onto the truth." Since colonial English terms such as "passive resistance" and "non-violent resistance" posed confusion amongst his followers, Gandhi avoided the use of these terms and persisted with the promotion of "Satyagraha." Against this background, we understand the story told elsewhere that, upon leaving for Sweden to receive the 1964 Nobel Peace Prize, Dr. Martin Luther King, Jr. is reported to have said that Dr. E. Stanley Jones' book on Mahatma Gandhi triggered his use of non-violence as a weapon for his own people's freedom in the United States.

Jones possessed a unique, open, and unabashed cross-cultural relationship of faith in Christ that enabled him to share and receive profound spiritual, social, and cultural persuasions from Indian cultural communities and their leaders. Much more needs to be done to fully understand Jones, and I am confident that *Thirty Days with E. Stanley Jones* will contribute to that conversation.

During this time of COVID-19, many people seek spiritual guidance to live with and overcome this dread disease and all of its implications. . In a global pandemic, healing the world depends on international solidarity for healing and wholeness of body, mind, and spirit. I look forward to this resource helping to create an "at-homeness" with God, with the Universe, with each other. I am sure nobody would refuse E. Stanley Jones' invitation to put our arms around the world and be healed from life's bruises.

Bishop Ivan Abrahams
General Secretary of the World Methodist Council, South Africa

Suggestions for Group Discussions

Scan this QR code with your mobile device or follow the link below to view a short group discussion video from the author:
youtu.be/1fvdrdqRiqE

The chapters in the book tend to follow Jones' life through his ministry and can easily be read and discussed in the order in which they are presented. However, some groups may desire a structure for a smaller number of gatherings which will deal with the subject material in a more organized way. The following outline for seven sessions clusters the readings around topics which might be of interest to groups.

Discussion 1:
Personal Faith Journey

Chapter 1: I Want What He Has

How did you first come to the faith? What were the "seed moments" in your faith journey?

Chapter 2: The Power of One

Who were the people who influenced your faith journey? When were you able to be the person who touched the life of another in their faith journey?

Chapter 4: A Log Jam of Wills

When did you have to make a difficult decision about the direction of your life? Where did you find guidance? Have you ever sensed "God's will" and how did you understand it?

Chapter 14: Life Reduced to Simplicity

If you were to express your central belief in one simple sentence, what would it be?

Chapter 15: Cardioversion Conversion

When have you experienced moments of deep insight, spiritual highs or experiences of the heart? What did they mean to you?

Chapter 24: Always Ascending

What are your dreams or goals for the future? Have there been times when you felt like you were going backward instead of forward? When have you experienced moments of "ascent"?

Chapter 25: Contagious, cosmic Laughter

Where do you find joy? Can you think of people you know who share a "contagious, cosmic laughter?"

Discussion 2:
Building Community: Ashrams and Roundtables

Chapter 16: The Ashram: Unreservedly, Unbreakably
Chapter 17. Here We Enter a Fellowship
Chapter 18. The Legacy of the Ashram

Share your experience of Christian community. Have there been times when the fellowship was broken? What "mottos" or values guide your life together? When have you felt you were truly welcomed by others in a community of caring?

Chapter 19. The Knights of the Round Table

What would it take to bring diverse sides—religiously, politically, socially—together at a roundtable? What are the practical applications of the Jones' model of the roundtable? In our day of deep divisions, is it even possible?

Discussion 3:
Interfaith Relations and Christian Unity

Chapter 11: Gandhi's word for Christians
Chapter 13: God's Trump Card

What can we learn from Gandhi's advice today? If Gandhi was "God's trump card" in the previous century, where is God's trump card being played today?

Chapter 10: Jesus isn't an American or a Brit

What images of Jesus speak to you about Universal Christ? Can you share some images from art, music or encounters with cultures other than your own which broaden your understanding of Christ?

Chapter 12: Living in the Tension

We live in a time of great tension and division. What can we learn from Gandhi and Jones about living in a time such as this? Can we hold differing points of view and divergent convictions in balance?

Can we grasp a vision of a universal, cosmic Christ which would overcome our political and religious divisions?

Chapter 20: Christians Unite

Jones' efforts at bringing the Christian denominations together did not succeed and the ecumenical movement of the 20th century has lost its energy. Where do you see signs of greater church unity or division? Is it possible for Christians to unite?

Discussion 4:
United Methodist History and Tradition

Chapter 1: I Want What He Has
Chapter 5: Experience and Expression

Have you had experience with Methodist traditions like camp meetings, revival services and altar calls? What events or "seed moments" shaped your life? What do you feel are the key characteristics of Methodism today?

Chapter 21: Methodism's Pink Fringe

Study the United Methodist Social Principles (www.umcjustice.org). What are the key elements of Methodism's social witness? How do you think the world views Methodism today?

Discussion 5:
Reconciliation, Racial Justice, the Role of Women and World Peace

Chapter 3: A Forming of Faith and Conscience

When did your sense of social conscience take shape? What were your early experiences with diversity and inclusion?

Chapter 7: Trail-blazing Women
Chapter 8: A Need I Had the Power of Meet

As we seek to live in community, what can we learn from the life of Mabel Lossing Jones? Who are some women who have been role models in the faith for you?

Chapter 6: The Day Democracy Died
Chapter 9: The Most Explosive Word

What do you think Jones would say about the Black Lives Matter movement? What progress have we made since his time and where are the roadblocks to racial justice?

Chapter 26: The World Still Waits
Chapter 27: Banned Books and Rebirth

What basic principles and beliefs guided Jones in his efforts for peace? Where do we see attempts at reconciliation and peace at work in the world today?

Discussion 6:
Dealing with Life, Health and Death

Chapter 22: Crisis of Health and Faith
Chapter 23: Falling into the Arms of Grace

At one time or another each of us deal with declining health, either our own or someone we love. Where do you find the resources to deal with life's disappointments and suffering?

Chapter 28: What About Death?

None of us like to think about death, but we all know the reality of it. Jones seemed to be able to face his own death unafraid. How can we do the same? Or can we?

Chapter 29: Saluting the Dawn with a Cheer

Jones offers what he believes will be the "last word." If you were to carve your own tombstone, what would it say? If you could choose one "last word" for your life, what would it be? What is your concept of what happens after death?

Discussion 7:
A Lasting Legacy

Chapter 30: I Can Still Hear His Voice
Chapter 31: Still Pretty Good

Reflect on what you have learned from the life of E. Stanley Jones. What do you feel his lasting legacy is today? What kind of a legacy would you like to leave behind? How do you want people to remember you?

Endnotes

Introduction

"In this country … " ESJ, *The Christ of the American Road*, page 70.

Preface

"He felt obliged …" Stephen Graham, *Ordinary Man, Extraordinary Mission*, page 10.

"Only Billy Graham …" *Time Magazine*, January 24, 1864, page 34.

"He was the most famous Christian missionary …" Henry Garman, *The Kingdom of God is a Wiser Radicalism*, Amazon Reviews, October 9, 2012.

"He was an unconventional Christian …" Stephen Graham, *Ordinary Man, Extraordinary Mission*, page 12.

"The issue was …" Naveen Rao, *History of 90 Years at Sat Tal Ashram*, page 1.

"Let us go out …" ESJ, "The Christ of the American Road", page 242.

"To preach the person of Jesus Christ …" ESJ, "The Christ of the American Road", page 52.

"The hesitation to give full equality …" ESJ, ibid, page 80, 243.

"Live in simplicity …" Naveen Rao, "History of 90 Years at Sat Tal Ashram", page 3.

Chapter 1: I want what he has

"Through his rough exterior …" ESJ, *Song of Ascents*, page 27.

"The third night came …" ibid, page 27.

"O spirit of God …" ESJ, *The Way to Power and Poise*, page 123.

Chapter 2: The Power of One

"The two boys …" Stephen Graham, *Ordinary Man, Extraordinary Mission*, page 23.

"Unveil the heart …" ibid, page 19.

"O Christ …" ESJ, *The Way*, page 302.

Chapter 3: A Forming of Faith and Conscience

"Desegregation was a God-given movement …" David Swartz, podcast, Asbury College chapel, January 21, 2015.

"Tension suffused Hughes Chapel …" David Swartz, *Facing West: American Evangelicals in an Age of World Christianity*, page 65.

"Resigned from board of trustees …" Robert Tuttle, *In Our Time*, page 234 and 317.

"In the southern states …" ESJ, *The Word Became Flesh*, page 251.

"Seldom have greater words …" ESJ, *The Christ of the American Road*, page 86-88.

"There is one thing …" ESJ, *Living Upon the Way*, page 105.

"O God …" ESJ, *The Way*, page 319.

Chapter 4: A Log Jam of Wills

"Had no notion…" ESJ, *Song of Ascents*, page 71.

"How surprised he was…" ibid, page 71-73 and *The Divine Yes*, page 68-69.

"I know so much …" Michael Lindvall, *Good News from North Haven*, page 80.

"Fifty years later …" ESJ, *The Divine Yes*, page 69.

"O God …" ESJ, *The Way*, page 281, 283.

Chapter 5: Experience and Expression

"If I were to pick …" ESJ, *Song of Ascents*, page 67.

"In the evening…" John Wesley's Journal, May 24, 1738.

"O blessed spirit…" ESJ, *Mastery*, page 128.

Chapter 6: The Day Democracy Died

"The moment I put my feet …" ESJ, *Song of Ascents*, page 256.

"You say I am guilty …" Robert Tuttle, *In Our Time*, page 234.

"O God who has made …" ESJ, *The Way*, page 319.

"Meeting in an unnamed city in the south …" ESJ, *The Christ of the American Road*, page 86.

"I saw in a newspaper …" ESJ, *The Word Made Flesh*, page 214.

"I am thankful …" ESJ, *The Divine Yes*, page 128.

"O Spirit of Truth …" ESJ, *The Way to Power and Poise*, page 135.

Chapter 7: Trail-blazing Women

"What are your plans …" Martha Chamberlain, *A Love Affair With India*, page 27.

"To attribute to one individual …" ibid, page 50.

"I suspect that few missionaries …" ibid, page 91.

"When Mabel was sent …" ibid, page 202.

"O Christ …" ESJ, *The Way*, page 360.

Chapter 8: A Need I had the Power to Meet

"By 1930 …" Stephen Graham, *Ordinary Man, Extraordinary Mission*, page 90.

"I became a missionary …" ibid, page 74.

"Bishop Frances Warren …" ibid, page 75.

"An early dinner …" ibid, page 85.

"Yes, I was tired …" *A Heart of Wisdom: The Long-awaited Journal of Mabel Lossing Jones*, page 243.

"O God …" ESJ, *The Way*, page 284.

Chapter 9: The Most Explosive Word

"When the Declaration of Independence …" ESJ, *The Christ of the American Road"* page 66.

"We have hesitated …" ibid, page 80.

"O God …" ESJ, *Mastery*, page 70.

Chapter 10: You Mean Jesus Isn't an American or a Brit?

"Burst like a bombshell …" Stephan Graham, *Ordinary Man, Extraordinary Mission*, page 12.

"His insight …" Steve Harper, *Insight: Surprised into Transformation*, Oboedire, October 5, 2019, page 13.

"One of the first ..." Robert Tuttle, *In Our Time*, page 93.

"All this happened ..." Steve Harper, ibid, page 14.

"O Spirit of God ..." ESJ, *The Way to Power and Poise*, page 134.

Chapter 11: Gandhi's Word to Christians

"What would you suggest ..." ESJ, *The Christ of the Indian Road*, page 118-120.

"Gandhi won the heart ..." Naveen Rao, personal correspondence, January, 2021.

"Jones was comfortable ..." E. Douglas Power and Jack Jackson, *E. Stanley Jones and Sharing the Good News in a Pluralistic Society*, page 117-119.

"O God ..." ESJ, *The Way*, page 331.

Chapter 12: Gandhi: Living in the Tension

"I am ashamed ..." ESJ, *Gandhi: Portrayal of a Friend*, page 11.

"a combination ..." ibid, page 17-34.

"Jones and Gandhi ..." Naveen Rao, personal correspondence, January 6, 2021.

"The church has failed ..." ESJ, *The Christ of the American Road*, page 222.

"O God ..." ESJ, *The Way to Power and Poise*, page 82.

Chapter 13: God's Trump Card

"So Mahatma Gandhi is ..." ESJ, *Gandhi: Portrayal of a Friend*, page 159-160.

"We have seen ..." ibid, page 157.

"Jones has rightly ..." Naveen Rao, personal correspondence, January 6, 2020.

"O Thou ..." ESJ, *The Way*, page 314.

Chapter 14: Life Reduced to Simplicity

"My faith ..." ESJ, *Song of Ascents*, page 352.

"As a last possible fling ..." ESJ, *The Unshakable Kingdom and the Unchanging Person*, page 11.

"When we say ..." ibid, page 52.

"The divine yes has sounded …" II Corinthians 1:19-20, Moffatt translation.

"O Christ …" ESJ, *Abundant Living*, page 186.

Chapter 15: Cardioversion Conversion

"A change in character and life …" ESJ, *Conversion*, page 16.

"Conversion is the law of life …" ibid, page 35.

"Soon the whole community …" ibid, page 39.

"Life impinging on life …" ibid, page 49.

"The Kingdom of God and The Way …" ibid, page 242.

"Then what is …" ibid, page 53.

"O Christ …" ESJ, *The Way*, page 124.

Chapter 16: The Ashram: Unreservedly, Unbreakable

"Of all the notes …" ESJ, *Song of Ascents*, page 233.

"We hadn't the slightest …" ibid, page 215.

"During this time …" Naveen Rao, *History of 90 Years at SatTal Ashram*, page 3.

"I expected to see …" ESJ, *Song of Ascents*, page 221.

"O Holy Spirit …" ESJ, *Mastery*, page 112.

Chapter 17: Here We Enter a Fellowship"

Photo: John E. Harnish

"The spirit of the Christian …" ESJ, *Along the Indian Road*, page 189.

"O Christ…" ESJ, *Mastery,* page 113.

Chapter 18: The Legacy of the Christian Ashram Today

"I really believe …" Tom Albin interview, June 2, 2020.

"The Christian Ashram culture …" ibid.

"It is clear to me …" ibid.

"O Holy Spirit …" ESJ, *The Way*, page 311.

Chapter 19: Knights of the Round Table

"The purpose was ..." ESJ, *Christ at the Round Table*, page 16.

"No one would argue ..." ibid, page 22.

"So that non-Christians ..." ESJ, *Song of Ascents*, page 237.

"Suppose the nations ..." ESJ, *Christ at the Round Table*, page 203.

"Gracious Father ..." ESJ, *Abundant Living*, page 199.

Chapter 20: Christians Unite!

"Christians are the most united ..." Stephen Graham, *Ordinary Man, Extraordinary Mission*, page 243.

"Christians Unite!" ibid.

"I missed a church ..." ibid, page 251.

"Gracious Father ..." ESJ, *Abundant Living*, page 202.

Chapter 21: Methodism's Pink Fringe"

"He may sound ..." Howard Snyder, *Profiles: E. Stanley Jones*, CatalystResources.org (http://www.catalystresources.org), March 1, 2010.

"What I saw in Russia ..." Robert Tuttle, *In Our Time*, page 164.

"Jones was prophetic ..." Howard Snyder, *Catalyst*, March 1, 2010.

"I am not a Communist ..." quoted by Henry Garman, *The Kingdom of God is a Wiser Radicalism*, Amazon Reviews, October 12, 2021 and Donna Bell Sanders, United Christian Ashram, June 5, 2021.

"O God ..." ESJ, *Abundant Living*, 220.

Chapter 22: A Crisis of Health and Faith

"Many missionaries ..." Robert Tuttle, *In Our Time*, page 71.

"He had not finished ..." ibid, page 74.

"Lord, I'm done for ..." ibid, page 80.

"O blessed Jesus ..." ESJ, *Mastery* page 175.

Chapter 23: Falling into the Arms of Grace

"Along the way..." ESJ, *The Divine Yes*, page 130-131.

"O God…" ESJ, *The Way*, page 31.

Chapter 24: Always Ascending

"I laugh at myself …" ESJ, *Song of Ascents*, page 15.

"I shall sing …" ibid, page 17-18.

"It is a song …" ibid, page 19.

"O God …" ESJ, *The Way to Power and Poise*, page 39.

Chapter 25: Contagious, Cosmic Laughter

"I was up …" *Living Upon the Way*, page 121.

"It is a paradox …" ibid, page 120.

"You have the most …" ESJ, *The Divine Yes*, page 125.

"I have often said …" ibid, page 149.

"O Christ …" ESJ, *The Way*, page 38.

Chapter 26: And the World Still Waits

"It should come …" Robert Tuttle, *In Our Time*, page 205.

"Probably no non-Indian …" *Encyclopedia of World Methodism*, vol. 1, page 1275.

"Churchmen's Campaign for Peace" https://archives.tricolib.brynmawr.edu/agents/corporate_entities/12083

"So I went …" ESJ, *Song of Ascents*, page 220-226.

"Did Stanley Jones …" Stephen Graham, *Ordinary Man, Extraordinary Mission*, page 264.

"Our best endeavors …" ESJ, *Song of Ascents*, page 202.

"O God …" ESJ, *The Way*, page 318.

Chapter 27: Banned Books and Rebirth

"I still remember …" Meeli Tankler, personal correspondence, January, 2021.

Photo: Courtesy of Rev. Lavere Webster, Wesley Collection, First United Methodist Church Birmingham, MI.

"I have held in my own hands ..." Meeli Tankler, personal correspondence, January 2021.

"O God ..." ESJ, *The Way*, page 332.

Chapter 28: And What About Death?

"So I stand assured ..." ESJ, *Song of Ascents*, page 368-369.

"If I keep ..." ibid, page 370.

"O Deathless Christ ..." ESJ, *The Way to Power and Poise*, page 157.

Chapter 29: Saluting the Dawn with a Cheer

"We went to the hospital ..." Charles Yoost, *Living the Abundant Life*, Sermon Nov. 3, 1974.

"Everyone may and can ..." ESJ, *Abundant Living*, page v.

"O Christ we thank thee ..." ibid, page 364.

"O Christ, I thank thee ..." ESJ, *The Way*, page 295.

Chapter 30: I Can Still Hear His Voice

"When I met ..." Clifford Bath, personal interview, September 2020.

"O Christ ..." ESJ, *The Way*, page 364.

Chapter 31: Still Pretty Good

"When he would visit our home ..." Sandy Sheppherd, personal correspondence, September 2020.

"When I was growing up ..." Mary John Dye, personal correspondence, September 2020.

"You can be rich ..." ESJ, *The Way*, page 290.

"You are in the hour ..." ibid, page 291.

"O Christ, I see ..." ESJ, *The Way*, page 291.

Works Cited

The following is a list of the resources I have cited in the book. In most cases, I am using early editions of E. Stanley Jones' works, many of which have been republished more than once. Therefore, page numbers may not correspond to more recent editions.

Books by E. Stanley Jones

The Christ of the American Road, 2020, E. Stanley Jones Foundation

A Song of Ascents, 1968, Abingdon Press

The Word Became Flesh, 1963, Abingdon Press

Mahatma Gandhi: An Interpretation, 1948, Abingdon Press

The Way, 1956, Abingdon Press

Abundant Living, 1952, Abingdon Press

The Way to Power and Poise, 1949, Abingdon Press

Mastery: The Art of Mastering Life, 1955, Abingdon Press

Along the Indian Road, 1939, Abingdon Press

Is the Kingdom of God Realism?, 1940, Abingdon Press

In Christ, 1961, Festival Books, Abingdon Press

Christ at the Round Table, 1928, Abingdon Press

The Christ of Every Road, 1930, Abingdon Press

The Christ of the Indian Road, 1925, Abingdon Press

The Divine Yes, 1975, Abingdon Press

The Unshakable Kingdom and the Unchanging Person, 1972, Abingdon Press

Works by other authors

Graham, Stephen, *Ordinary Man, Extraordinary Mission: The Life and Works of E. Stanley Jones*, 2005, Abingdon Press

Tuttle, Robert G., *In Our Time: The Life and Ministry of E. Stanley Jones*, 2019, E. Stanley Jones Foundation

Mathews, James K. and Eunice Jones Mathews, *Selections from E. Stanley Jones: Christ and Human Need*, 1972, Abingdon Press

Chamberlain, Martha Gunsalus, *A Love Affair with India: The Story of the Wife and Daughter of E. Staley Jones*, 2018, E. Stanley Jones Foundation

Powe, F. Douglas and Jack Jackson, *E. Stanley Jones and Sharing the Good News in a Pluralistic Society*, 2018, Wesley's Foundry Books, General Board of Higher Education and Ministry

Mathews-Younes, Anne, *Living Upon the Way: Selected Sermons of E. Stanley Jones on Self-surrender*, 2008, Lucknow Publishing House

Rao, Principal Naveen, *90th Year of Sat Tal Christian Ashram, Nov. 7, 2020*, and personal correspondence, Leonard Theological College, Jabalpur, India

Christian History Magazine, #136, 2020, Church History Institute

Swartz, David, *Facing West: American Evangelicals in an Age of World Religions*, Oxford University Press, 2020.

Yoost, Charles, *Living the Abundant Life*, sermon, November 3, 1974

Snyder, Howard, *Profiles: E. Stanley Jones, Mission and Evangelism*, March 1, 2010, https://www.catalystresources.org

Hendershot, Kathryn Reese, *E. Stanley Jones Had a Wife: The Life and Missiological Contributions of Dr. Mabel Lossing Jones*, https://www.Asburyseminary.edu/ecommonsatsdissertations

Harper, Steve, *Insight: Surprised by Transformation*, https://www.Oboedire.wordpress.com, October 5, 2019

Thurman, Howard, *With Head and Heart: The Autobiography of Howard Thurman*, 1979, Harcourt Brace Jovanovich Publishers

Mathews-Younes, Anne, *A Heart of Wisdom: The Long-awaited Journal of Mabel Lossing Jones*, E. Stanley Jones Foundation, 2021

Unless otherwise noted, photos are from the Archives and Special Collections of the B.L. Fisher Library, Asbury Theological Seminary, Wilmore, KY or the E. Stanley Jones Foundation and are used with permission.

About the Author

Rev. Dr. John E. Harnish is an ordained United Methodist pastor, the Pastor Emeritus at First United Methodist Church, Birmingham, MI. A native of Clarion, PA, he was ordained in the Western Pennsylvania Conference of the UMC and served churches in Western Pennsylvania and Michigan, including First UMC Ann Arbor, MI and First UMC Birmingham, MI.

For seven years, he was the Associate General Secretary for the General Board of Higher Education and Ministry of the United Methodist Church. In that role, he worked with seminaries and programs of clergy education and was involved in the work of the World Methodist Council around the world.

He has served on the Boards of Trustees for the Methodist Theological School in Ohio, Adrian College and the Baltic Methodist Theological Seminary in Estonia. In 2022, Dr. Harnish was awarded the "Frances Asbury Award" by the Michigan Conference of the United Methodist Church. The award is given by the General Board of Higher Education and Ministry to a person who has made significant contributions to United Methodist ministry of higher education and campus ministry.

As a writer, he has published two previous books, *The Orders of Ministry in the United Methodist Church* and *Do Not Be Afraid: Bishops and Young Clergy Share Signs of Resurrection and Words of Hope.* He is a frequent columnist for *MIConnect*, the Michigan UM online magazine and the *Record Patriot* newspaper in addition to his weekly blog "Monday Memo" which can be found at JackHarnish.wordpress.com. In 2019 he received the Donn Doten Award of Excellence from the United Methodist Association of Communicators.

A graduate of Asbury College and Asbury Theological Seminary, he received an honorary Doctor of Divinity degree from Garrett-Evangelical Theological Seminary and was awarded the Eliza Garrett Distinguished Service Award in 2013.

Jack, as he is often known, is married to Judith Harnish. They have two sons who are both in education and he makes his home on Platte Lake in Northern Michigan.

You can follow Dr. Harnish's work or invite him to Zoom with your small group by visiting his website, JohnEHarnish.com.

About the E. Stanley Jones Foundation

The E. Stanley Jones Foundation is dedicated to preserving and extending the legacy of the late E. Stanley Jones. The foundation's mission is to distribute the writing and resources of E. Stanley Jones in order to build the Kingdom of God. The foundation works with universities, churches, and individuals.

The Foundation continues to publish books today to fulfill E. Stanley Jones' vision. Visit EStanleyJonesFoundation.com for more information, photo galleries, additional resources, and the latest book releases, including:

Selections from Christ and Human Need by E. Stanley Jones

Christian Maturity by E. Stanley Jones

A Heart of Wisdom: The Long-awaited Diary of Mabel Lossing Jones compiled and edited by Anne Mathews-Younes

Christ and Human Suffering by E. Stanley Jones

The Reconstruction of the Church by E. Stanley Jones

Quotations included in *Thirty Days with E. Stanley Jones* from E. Stanley Jones' writing were provided by The E. Stanley Jones Foundation and are used with permission.

More in the *Thirty Days With* series

Thirty Days with Abraham Lincoln

by Duncan Newcomer

Abraham Lincoln is the soul of America, calling us to our best as Americans. Duncan Newcomer has hosted more than 200 episodes of the radio series Quiet Fire: The Spiritual Life of Abraham Lincoln. Now, 30 of his best stories provide a month of inspirational reading.

Thirty Days with King David

by Larry Buxton

In turbulent times, King David united a nation—and his hard-earned wisdom can bring us together today. In this book, pastor, educator and leadership coach Larry Buxton shows us how David embodies 14 crucial values shared by effective leaders to this day.

Thirty Days with America's High School Coaches

by Martin Davis

High school coaches shape millions of lives. These 30 true stories show how coaches nationwide combine imagination, wisdom and selfless commitment to prepare teens to meet the future.

CPSIA information can be obtained
at www.ICGtesting.com
Printed in the USA
JSHW040947171222
35065JS00005B/19

9 781641 801317